Matthias Nace Forney

Political Reform by the Representation of Minorities

Matthias Nace Forney

Political Reform by the Representation of Minorities

ISBN/EAN: 9783337070588

Printed in Europe, USA, Canada, Australia, Japan

Cover: Foto ©Suzi / pixelio.de

More available books at **www.hansebooks.com**

POLITICAL REFORM

BY THE

Representation of Minorities

MATTHIAS N. FORNEY

———————

NEW YORK:
PUBLISHED BY THE AUTHOR AT 47 CEDAR ST.
1894.

CONTENTS.

PREFACE.

When the compilation of the following pages was commenced the intention was first, to describe briefly the evils growing out of the present system of electing, by a majority or plurality of the votes cast in each district, single members to represent the people in it, in national, state or municipal legislative assemblies; second, to show that by increasing the size of or consolidating a number of the present districts and electing several members from each, by a system which would give minorities as well as majorities representation, at least some of these evils would be remedied; third, to give a very brief, simple, and as clear an explanation as possible of what is meant by minority, proportional or personal representation—as it has been called by different writers—then to collect from the various books and essays on the subject some of the most convincing arguments which have been advanced in favor of adopting some such method of electing representatives to our national, state, and municipal legislative bodies.

In making such an explanation the practice which has prevailed in Illinois, for more than twenty years, of choosing the members of the House of Representatives in that State by a system of cumulative voting, afforded an object lesson from which the general principles of the simplest form of minority representation could be described and made obvious to those who are totally ignorant of the subject—and at least nineteen-twentieths of all who are ordinarily regarded as intelligent people are included in this class—more easily than in any other way. As the Illinois system was used as an illustration, it was thought readers would naturally ask how it has worked in practice. To answer this anticipated inquiry a method of getting information was adopted which has been used very successfully in various associations with which the writer has been connected, for making investigations relating to technical subjects. This method is to prepare a series of questions framed with a view to eliciting the kind of information which is wanted, and then print them in the form of a circular of inquiry, and send copies of it to those who are likely to be possessed of the information or experience which is desired and solicit replies to the questions. This was done and answers were received from persons in all parts of the State of Illinois, to whom the circular was sent, giving their opinions and the results of their observation and experience, with reference to the practical working of the system of electing representatives to the legislature of that State. The information thus obtained indicated the merits and also some of the defects of the Illinois system of election. This led to investigations for remedies for the defects indicated and extended the scope of the following pages much beyond the purpose with which their compilation was commenced.

It has been said that notwithstanding the fact that minority representation has been discussed for nearly half a century, that the system has secured but a limited adoption, probably because "no entirely satisfactory plan has been proposed." The final object aimed at in the following pages was to explain a system which it is thought would be "satisfactory" and to set forth the reasons for that belief.

The writer feels that a word of apology is due to himself, on account of the haste with which the book has been prepared. All the work has been done in time which could be taken from the exacting duties of editing a technical paper. While he has not consciously "depended upon his imagination for his facts," he has often relied upon his memory and quotations for his arguments. The abundance of quotations, in fact, leaves little room for any claims of authorship, but only for such as a compiler may make. In the latter capacity free use has been made of the contributions of other writers on the subjects of these pages, many of which are scattered through periodicals and are thus difficult of access to the general reader. These quotations were made because the facts and the arguments contained therein were set forth with much greater force and clearness than the writer could hope to command, and such quotations have often the additional weight which is added by the names of distinguished authors.

The immediate purpose of the book was to present its subject to the consideration of the members of the Constitutional Convention of this State who are assembling at the same time that this preface is being written. To accomplish that purpose it should now be in the hands of those who are to revise the organic law of the State of New York. It was only by the most incessant work that it was brought as near to completion as it now is. Its purpose requires that it be launched at once with whatever defects it has—and many will doubtless become obvious when it will be too late to retrieve them.

Persons interested in the reform proposed in the following pages, and disposed to give their aid and countenance to secure its adoption, are invited to send their names and addresses to the writer.

M. N. FORNEY.

47 Cedar Street, New York.

May 8, 1894.

POLITICAL REFORM

BY THE

REPRESENTATION OF MINORITIES.

CHAPTER I.

REPRESENTATION.

With the struggle for civil liberty there has always been a contest for the representation of the people in legislative bodies. During the colonial period of our existence disputes of this kind were frequent and to-day, in the great city of New York and in other places where a great part—and often the best part—of the people are deprived of adequate representation in the municipal, state, and national government the strife is still continued. A standing grievance in labor strikes is that the representatives of the laborers are not " recognized " and the interests of the men are thus without satisfactory representation. In the first written charter granted in 1606 to the colony which was planted in Virginia, we are told * that none of the rights of self-government or elements of popular government nor the elective franchise was introduced into the form of government, and that the fruits thereof were tyranny, confusion, oppression, poverty and suffering.

Contrasted with the results of this misrepresentative form of government it is said that in 1619 Sir George Yeardley arrived in the Virginia colony with " commissions and instructions from the company for the better establishinge of a commonwealth." It provided " that the planters might have a hande in the governing of themselves, yet was graunted that a generall assemblie shoulde be helde yearly once, whereat were to be present the governor and counsell with two burgesses from each plantation, freely to be elected by the inhabitants

*Bancroft's " History of the United States."

thereof, this assemblie to have power to make and ordaine whatsoever laws and orders should by them be thought good and profitable for their subsistence.''

This charter '' had the general assent and the applause of the whole assemblie, with thanks for it to Almighty God and to those from whom it had issued, in the names of the burgesses and of the whole colony whom they represented.''

Of this charter Bancroft says : ''A perpetual interest attaches to this first elective body that ever assembled in the Western world, representing the people of Virginia, and making laws for their government, more than a year before the *Mayflower*, with the Pilgrims, left the harbor of Southampton.''

In 1621 a written constitution was established for the colony creating a general assembly to consist of the members of the council, and of two burgesses to be chosen from each of the several plantations by the respective inhabitants.   The historian's comments on this are : '' The system of *representative* government thus became in the new hemisphere an acknowledged right. * * *   It constituted the plantation, in its infancy, a nursery of freemen ; and succeeding generations learned to cherish institutions which were as old as the first period of the prosperity of their fathers.''

In Massachusetts it is recorded that '' for more than eighteen years ' the whole body of the male inhabitants ' constituted the legislature ; the state was governed like our towns as a strict democracy. * * *   At length the increase of population, and its diffusion over a wider territory, led to the introduction of the *representative* system, and each town sent its committee to the general court.''

In 1639 the first assembly of Maryland framed a declaration of rights, which '' established a system of *representative* government.''

The charter granted to Roger Williams in 1644 gave to the people in Rhode Island '' full power and authority to rule themselves.''   It asserted that '' all men were equal ; all might meet and debate in the public assemblies ; all might aspire to office ; the people for a season constituting itself its own tribune, and every public law required confirmation in the primary assemblies.''

In his book on '' Representative Government and Personal Representation," Mr. Simon Sterne refers to "the remarkable degree to which the ideas of representative government and free institutions were developed in the colony of New Netherland as early as 1645. By the eighth clause of the instructions of the commissioners of the Assembly of XIX, relative to the government of the colony, it was declared that ' Further, inasmuch as the respective colonists have been allowed by the freedoms to delegate one or two persons to give information to the Director and Council at least once a year, of the state and condition of their colonies, the same is hereby confirmed.'*

"That the colonists were not contented with the simple right 'to give information,' but demanded a representative form of government, is indicated by the petition of the commonalty of New Netherland, etc., to Director Stuyvesant, in the year 1653, of which the fourth clause contains the following very remarkable words :

" ' Tis contrary to the first intentions and general principles of every well-regulated government that one or more men should arrogate to themselves the exclusive power to dispose at will, of the life and property of any individual, and this by virtue, or under pretense of a law or order, he or they might enact, without the consent, knowledge, or election of the whole body, or its agents or representatives.

" ' Hence the enactment of new laws or orders affecting the community or inhabitants, their lives or property, is contrary and opposed to the granted freedoms of the Dutch government, and odious to every free-born man, and principally so to those whom God has placed in a free state or on newly-settled lands, which might require new laws or orders, not transcending, but resembling as near as possible, those of Netherland. We humbly submit that it is one of our privileges that our consent, *or that of our representatives*, is necessarily required in the enactment of such laws and orders.' " *

In reviewing these events Bancroft says : " In the early history of the United States, nothing is more remarkable than the uniform attachment of each colony to its franchises ; and popular assemblies burst everywhere into life with a consciousness of their importance, and an immediate capacity for efficient legislation."

---

* "Documents relating to the Colonial History of the State of New York." Vol. I. pp. 499, 550.

In the management of their local affairs during the colonial period it was, then, a struggle for *representation* and every student of our early history must be impressed with the fact that, in the long contest with the mother country, which began soon after the first settlement on this side of the Atlantic, and ended with our revolutionary war, it was always a contest for this right.

Just prior to the revolution in an examination before a committee of the House of Commons, in England, Franklin testified as follows:

"An internal tax is forced from the people *without* their consent, if not laid by their *representatives.* * * * The Americans think it extremely hard and unjust, that a body of men, in which they have no *representatives*, should make a merit to itself of giving and granting what is not its own, but theirs; and deprive them of a right they esteem of the utmost value and importance, as it is the security of all their other rights. * * *

"As to an internal tax, how small soever, laid by the legislature here on the people there, while they have no *representatives* in this legislature, I think it will never be submitted to. * * *

"They (the people) find in the Great Charter, and the Petition and Declaration of Rights, that one of the privileges of English subjects is, that they are not to be taxed but by their common consent; they have therefore relied upon it, from the first settlement of the province, that the Parliament never would, nor could, by color of that clause in the charter, assume a right of taxing them, till it had qualified itself to exercise such right, by admitting representatives from the people to be taxed, who ought to make a part of that common consent." * * *

This sentiment was finally formulated during our contest with Britain in the acclamation of "No Taxation without Representation," and partly under its incitement the historical cargo of tea was thrown overboard in Boston harbor.

The banners which have been carried in the conflicts for liberty in the past have always had inscribed on them a demand for *representation*, and at the present day the question of representation is often the real one at issue in labor strikes and sometimes forms the chief obstacle which stands in the way of amicable agreement and the settlement of disputes between employers and their men. At the critical period of a recent strike on a railroad, the following notice was issued by the president of the company :

" *To all employés :*

" To correct any misapprehension regarding the position of the officers of this company I would state that they are at all times ready and willing to give patient hearing to complaints on the part of its employés, or any number of them, in any department. If dissatisfied with the conclusions reached by the division superintendents or general superintendent, the President will hear their cases and decide, but we decline to confer with organized committees composed of several branches of the service, for the reason that we cannot know that such committees fairly represent its employés. Engineers cannot, of course, fairly represent grievances of telegraph men, nor can firemen properly represent trainmen."

It will be seen that in this " notice " there were several collateral issues involved and whether the President would have " recognized " committees who " fairly" represented the employés, or whether he would have acknowledged the right of the latter to select their own representatives are probably questions which were not then decided, but will be sure to continue to come up until some equitable decision is reached. Among the commonest—and it may be added—often the *righteous* " grievances " of workingmen is the refusal of employers to " recognize " or treat with the committees who have been appointed by the men to represent their interests, and probably the recognition of this *right of representation* would in times past have done, and would do much in the future to avoid these contests which, in modern times, are so detrimental to the interests of both the parties engaged therein.

While representing the American cause in England it is reported that Franklin in an interview with a distinguished English statesman said, " It seems to me that every body of men who cannot appear in person should have a right to appear by an agent " (or representative). The right of representation could not be more concisely or forcibly stated and the doctrine is applicable to all our relations, be they political, social or industrial.

What may be called the philosophy—or perhaps better—the ethics of representation, in civil government, is elucidated with remarkable clearness and conclusiveness in Guizot's " History of Representative Government," and at the risk of a long quotation the following extract from that book is reprinted here :

" Starting from the principle that truth, reason and justice,—in one word, the divine law,—alone possess rightful power, the reasoning of the true doctrine of representation is somewhat as follows :—Every society, according to its interior organization, its antecedents, and the aggregate influences which have or still do modify it, is placed to a certain extent in a position to apprehend truth and justice as the divine law, and is in a measure disposed to conform itself to this law. Employing less general terms—there exists in every society a certain number of just ideas and wills in harmony with these ideas, which respect the reciprocal rights of men and social relations with their results. This sum of just ideas and loyal wills is dispersed among the individuals who compose society, and unequally diffused among them on account of the infinitely varied causes which influence the moral and intellectual development of men. The grand concern, therefore, of society is—that, so far as either abiding infirmity or the existing condition of human affairs will allow, this power of reason, justice and truth, which alone has an inherent legitimacy, and alone has the right to demand obedience, may become prevalent in the community, The problem evidently is to collect from all sides the scattered and incomplete fragments of this power that exist in society, to concentrate them, and form them, to constitute a government. In other words, it is required to discover all the elements of legitimate power that are disseminated throughout society, and to organize them into an actual power ; that is to say, to collect into one focus, and to realize, public reason and public morality, and to call them to the occupation of power.

" What we call *representation* is nothing else than a means to arrive at this result,—it is not an arithmetical machine employed to collect and count individual wills, but a natural process by which public reason, which alone has a right to govern society, may be extracted from the bosom of society itself. No reason has in fact a right to say beforehand for itself that it is the reason of the community. If it claims to be such, it must prove that it is so, that is to say, it must accredit itself to other individual reasons which are capable of judging it. If we look at facts, we shall find that all institutions, all conditions of the representative system, flow from and return to this point. Election, publicity, and responsibility, are so many tests applied to individual reasons, which in the search for, or in the exercise of, power, assume to be the interpreters of the reason of the community ; so many means of bringing to light the elements of legitimate power, and preventing usurpation.

" In this system, it is true—and the fact arises from the necessity of liberty as actual in the world—that truth and error, perverse and loyal wills, in one word, the good and evil which co-exist and contend in society as in the individual, will most probably express themselves ; this is the condition of the world ; it is the necessary result of liberty. But against the evil of this there are two guarantees : one is found in the publicity of the struggle, which always gives the right the best chance of success, for it has been recognized in all ages of the world that good is in friendship with the light, while evil ever shelters itself in darkness ; this idea, which is common to all the religions of the world, symbolizes and indicates the first of all truths. The second guarantee consists in the determination of a certain amount of capacity to be possessed by those who aspire to exercise any branch of power. In the system of representing wills, nothing could justify such a limitation, for the will exists full and entire in all men, and confers on all men an equal right ; but the limitation flows necessarily from the principle which attributes power to reason and not to will.

* * * * *

" So far then from representation founding itself on the right, inherent in all individual wills, to concur in the exercise of power, it on the other hand rests on the principle that no will has in itself any right to power, and that whoever exercises, or claims to exercise power, is bound to prove that he exercises, or will exercise it, not according to his own will but according to reason. If we examine the representative system in all its forms, * * * we shall see that such are everywhere the necessary results and the true foundations of that which we call representation."

The principle which attributes power to reason and not to will and that a certain amount of *capacity* should be possessed by those who aspire to exercise any branch of power, has been recognized in our various kinds of government, national, state and municipal. In the State of New York every male citizen of the age of twenty-one years, who has been a resident in his district and state a certain length of time, is of a sound mind and who has not bribed or been bribed at or made a bet on the elections, or been convicted of an infamous crime can vote. The question whether this is the wisest discrimination which could be made between those who are assumed *to have* and those who *have not* the "capacity" for exercising the power which the franchise gives will not be discussed now. The fact is this is the discrimination which has been made not only in the State of New York but is substantially the same in nearly all the other states in the Union. It was said half a century ago " that the notion that in any large community, government is the creation of the *whole* people, or that it has in any proper sense, received the assent of all, is entirely fanciful. The truth is, that even in the most favorable cases, but a comparatively small portion of the people have actually any share in directing the affairs of state ; and of that portion, a bare majority, as will be shown, and often less, may usually prescribe the form and policy of the government, under which all are to live, and to which all are held equally bound to render obedience. More than three-fourths of the entire population are excluded by reason of their sex, age, or other declared disqualification, from all participation in the right of voting. The exclusion is somewhat arbitrary ; indeed, no more is pretended than that it proceeds upon a general presumption of unfitness which is adopted for the sake of convenience." *

In other words, in effect, it is asserted by the Constitution and Laws of nearly all the states, that the persons described have the "capacity" required or are *qualified* for the exercise of the power which the franchise gives, and by inference it would follow that those not embraced by the conditions, which have been enacted into law, have not the capacity and are in fact *disqualified*. This discrimina-

---

* From " An Elementary Treatise on the Structure and Operation of the National and State Governments of the United States," by Charles Mason, A. M.

tion places very great limitations on the definition of our system of government as " Government of the People, by the People, and for the People."

Interpreted in accordance with our legislation this formula is now accurately expressed as Government of and for all the People by those declared to be qualified. The " Sovereignty of the People " in New York and other states really means the Sovereignty of the Male Citizens of the age of twenty-one years, who have been Residents in their Districts and States, a certain length of time, are of Sound Minds and have not Bribed or been Bribed at nor made Bets in Elections or been convicted of an Infamous Crime. The phrase the " Sovereignty of the People " then in an American community really means, what may be expressed, as the *Sovereignty of the " Qualified."* Paraphrasing Guizot's language slightly our theory then is that " representation is a means of collecting from all sides the scattered and incomplete fragments of the power of reason, justice and truth that exist among the ' Qualified ' voters, to concentrate them and collect them into one focus and call them to the occupation of power." This theory should include the right of the " Qualified " " to appear by an agent" or representative, which Franklin declared "every body of men who cannot appear in person had," and which those of us, whom the law says are qualified to vote, somewhat vaguely and, as we will try to show, often *erroneously* imagine we possess. The Sovereignty of the Qualified is the theory, but under existing practice and the present administration of affairs the result is often very different, and as has been said a bare majority of those qualified to vote—*often less*— " may prescribe the form and policy of the government, under which all are held equally bound to render obedience."

CHAPTER II

To show how a minority may govern the *a priori demonstration* given by Mr. Alfred Cridge of San Francisco in a little pamphlet on Proportional Representation, will be given. In this he says :

"It can be demonstrated, aside from any actual experience, that under representation by districts, minorities, from one-third down (the proportion growing less with the increased number of parties), can return a majority of the members in elective bodies."

He then gives the following illustrations of this—suppose three constituencies or districts having 3000 voters each, select each a member to a representative body, and that the voters in the different districts are divided between the two dominant parties as shown in the following table :

DISTRICTS.	VOTERS.		REPRESENTATIVES ELECTED.
	REPUBLICANS.	DEMOCRATS.	
First	2,000	1,000	Republican.
Second	2,000	1,000	Republican.
Third.		3,000	Democrat.
Total Votes....	4,000	5,000	

It is obvious that with such a division of voters that in the first and second districts Republicans would be elected, and in the third a Democrat. The total number of Republican voters in the three districts is 4000 while the Democrats number 5000 so that we would have the anomaly and the injustice of having 4000 Republicans represented by two members while 5000 Democrats have only one, and yet this may

and does occur under our present system which is based on the principle that "the majority should rule."

Another illustration with seven districts each having ·7000 voters
is cited by Mr. Cridge:

| DISTRICTS. | VOTERS. | | REPRESENTATIVES |
	REPUBLICANS.	DEMOCRATS.	ELECTED.
First	3,000	4,000	Democrat.
Second	3,000	4,000	Democrat.
Third	3,000	4,000	Democrat.
Fourth	3,000	4,000	Democrat.
Fifth	7,000		Republican.
Sixth. ,.......	7,000		Republican.
Seventh	7,000		Republican.
Total Votes....	33,000	16,000	

In this case 33,000 Republicans would have only *three* representatives while 16,000 Democrats would have *four*, that is less than a third
of the voters in the seven districts would elect a majority of the representatives.

Mr. Cridge gives still another illustration of seven districts each
with 7000 voters but divided among three parties, as shown on page 16.

Here we again have 49,000 voters in seven districts. The Populists with 12,000—*less than a fourth* of the whole—would get a majority of the representatives, while the Democrats with 17,000 votes
get none. Mr. Cridge says:

"It may be claimed that the cases represented are extreme. But
there are other factors, of which we have so far taken no cognizance,
that will still further increase disparities. It is practically impossible
for voters in a mass to control party management; and a very small
minority in the party not only can, but do, not only do, but must,

| DISTRICTS. | VOTERS. | | | REPRESENTA- |
	REPUBLICANS.	DEMOCRATS.	POPULISTS.	TIVES ELECTED.
First	2,000	2,000	3,000	Populist.
Second.......	2,000	2,000	3,000	Populist.
Third.......	2,000	2,000	3,000	Populist.
Fourth	2,000	2,000	3,000	Populist.
Fifth.........	4,000	3,000		Republican.
Sixth.........	4,000	3,000		Republican.
Seventh	4,000	3,000		Republican.
Total Votes...	20,000	17,000	12,000	

control the nominations, so that the option (not choice) of the voter, in most cases, is to vote for one man that does not represent him in preference to voting for another that would misrepresent him. If his party wins, he is therefore misrepresented ; if it loses he is misrepresented."

It will thus be seen that the results of elections depend very much upon how districts are divided. Politicians have not been slow to avail themselves of this means of influencing and controlling the results of elections. Such division of districts, for the advantage of one party over another, is an evil inherent in the present system of electing representatives, and has long been known as gerrymandering, and is defined in Webster's dictionary as " the division (of a state) into districts for the choice of representatives, in an unnatural and unfair way, with a view to give a political party an advantage over its opponent."*

---

*The following description and illustration of the origin of this term is taken from the *American Law Review* for January, 1872 :

"The term Gerrymander, as it is well known, dates from the year 1811, when Elbridge Gerry was Governor of Massachusetts, and the Democratic, or, as it was then

In the report on Representation Reform made to the United States Senate in 1869, of which Mr. Buckalew was chairman, it was said :

"Single districts will almost always be unfairly made. They will be formed in the interest of party and to secure an unjust measure of power to their authors, and it may be expected that each successive district apportionment will be more unjust than its predecessor. Parties

---

termed, the Republican party, obtained a temporary ascendency in the state. In order to secure themselves in the possession of the government, the party in power passed the famous law of Feb. 11, 1812, providing for a new division of the state into senatorial districts, so contrived that in as many districts as possible the Federalists should be outnumbered by their opponents. To effect this all natural and customary lines were disregarded, and some parts of the state, particularly the counties of Worcester and Essex, presented singular examples of political geography. It is said that

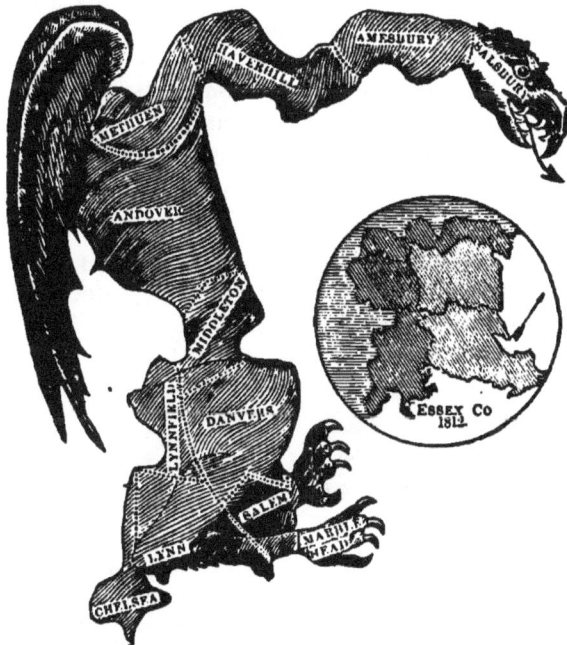

Gilbert Stuart, seeing in the office of the *Columbian Centinel* an outline of the Essex outer district, nearly encircling the rest of the county, added with his pencil a beak to Salisbury, and claws to Salem and Marblehead, as shown in the engraving exclaiming "There that will do for a salamander." "Salamander," said Mr. Russell, the editor, " I call it a Gerry-mander." The *mot* obtained vogue and a rude cut

will retaliate upon each other whenever possible. The disfranchisement suffered through one decade by a political party may be repeated
upon it in the next with increased severity, but if it shall happen to
have power in the legislature when the new apportionment for the state
is to be made, it will take signal vengeance for its wrongs and in its
turn indulge in the luxury of persecution.''

In a speech made in Philadelphia in 1867 he said what is probably
just as true now that "at this moment, from the British possessions
on the northeast to the Golden Gate of the Pacific, there is probably
not an honest apportionment law for members of Congress, and you will
scarcely ever have one, unless in an exceptional case where one political interest shall have control of the upper branch of a legislature and
another of the lower, holding each other in check, and compelling
some degree of fairness in the formation of law.''

As Prof. Commons in a paper on this subject said, "public opinion cannot stop the gerrymander, because public opinion rejoices in
this kind of tit-for-tat. The fact that one party has unfavorably cut
up the state is good reason for the other party to retrieve itself when it
gets the power. If Congress should take the matter out of the hands of
the state legislature, it would be simply to do its own gerrymandering,
while state and municipal gerrymandering would still go on as before.''

But it is not alone by gerrymandering that injustice is done through
our present system of electing single members by a majority of votes in
each district. The literature on this subject is full of glaring examples
of unfairness and violation of the principle that a Majority of Qualified
Voters should Rule.

The language used by President Garfield in the course of a remarkable speech before the House of Representatives, in 1870, in support

---

of the figure published in the *Centinel*, and in the *Salem Gazette*, with the natural
history of the monster duly set forth, served to fix the word in the political vocabulary
of the country. So efficient was the law that at the elections of 1812, 50,164 Democratic voters elected twenty-nine senators against eleven elected by 51,766 Federalists;
and Essex county, which, when voting as a single district, had sent five Federalists
to the Senate, was now represented in that body by three Democrats and two Federalists. It was repealed in 1814, and the death and burial of the monster were
celebrated in prose and verse throughout the country.''

of a motion for the election of congressmen by the cumulative vote has often been quoted. He then said :

" When I was first elected to Congress in the fall of 1862 the State of Ohio had a clear Republican majority of about 25,000, but by the adjustment and distribution of political power in the state there were fourteen Democratic representatives upon this floor and only five Republicans. The state that cast nearly 250,000 Republican votes as, against 225,000 Democratic votes was represented in the proportion of five Republicans and fourteen Democrats.

" In the next Congress there was no great political change in the popular vote of Ohio—a change of only 20,000—but the result was that seventeen Republican members were sent here from Ohio and only two Democrats.

" We find that only so small a change as 20,000 changed the representatives in Congress from fourteen Democrats and five Republicans to seventeen Republicans and two Democrats.

" Now, no man, whatever his politics, can justly defend a system that may in theory and frequently does in practice, produce such results as these."

Again he said :

" In my judgment it is the weak point in the theory of representative government as now organized and administered, that a large portion of the people are permanently disfranchised. There are about 30,000 Democratic voters in my district, and they have been voting for the last forty years without any more hope of gaining a representative on this floor than of having one in the Commons of Great Britain."

In an Address to the Public, which the American Proportional Representation League issued at the time the Proportional Representation Congress was held in Chicago last summer (1893), it is said :

" Twenty-three years have been added to the forty and still the Democrats of that district maintain the forlorn hope. Iowa with 219,215 Republican votes and 201,923 Democratic votes at the election of 1892, sent ten Republican congressmen and one Democrat to Washington. Every 21,921 Republicans of that state has a representative, while the whole 201,923 Democrats have but one. In Kentucky the case is reversed. The Democrats have a congressman for every 17,436 votes, while the Republicans have one for 122,308. In Maine the vote was 65,637 Republicans and 55,778 Democrats, but the Republicans got all the four congressmen. In Maryland the vote was 91,762 Republicans and 113,931 Democrats, but the latter got the six congressmen. The Republicans of Texas have not had a representative in Congress since 1882. The Democrats of Kansas have not had a representative since the state was admitted to the Union, though they have polled from a third to two-fifths of the vote of the state during that time.''

To show further how the majority system works in practice an ordinary district in the State of New York in which a member of the legislature is to be elected may be taken as an illustration. We will select the vote for member of Assembly at the election in 1892 in Herkimer county, New York, where 6140 Republican, 5629 Democratic and 402 Prohibition votes were cast. The Republican candidate of course was elected, and the 6140 voters of that faith were represented, whereas the 5629 Democrats and 402 Prohibitionists were unrepresented. That is, the Republicans in that county had some one in the legislature to advocate those views and measures concerning which they differed from their political antagonists, whereas the Democrats and Prohibitionists had not. To show the relative proportion of the votes of the two parties clearly the Republican vote is represented by the parallelogram or area R in Fig. 1, shaded with diagonal lines, and the Democratic vote by the black area D. The Prohibitionist vote is shown by the small area indicated by the letter P, and which is shaded by cross lines. The horizontal length of these areas represents correctly to a scale the magnitude of the respective votes.

In Montgomery county a similar condition of things existed, 5590

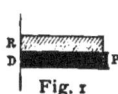

Fig. 1

Fig. 2

Democratic voters, represented by the shaded area D in Fig. 2, elected three candidates, and 5587 Republican votes, shown by the black area R, and 377 Prohibition votes, P were unrepresented. It will be seen from the diagram and also from the figures that in this latter case the Republican and Prohibition votes added together exceed those of the

Democrats, so that a *minority* of the voters in this county elected the candidate.

To show the extent to which the qualified voters in the State of New York were unrepresented, after the election held in 1892, a diagram, Fig. 3, p. 22, has been drawn, in which the magnitude of the votes cast by the different parties in each district is represented by parallelograms as in Figs. 1 and 2. These are correctly drawn to a scale, the successful votes being represented by the areas shaded with single diagonal lines and the unsuccessful votes by the black areas. The scattering votes are shown by the small areas, on the ends of the black areas, and which, as in Figs. 1 and 2, are shaded by cross lines. The relative proportion of the successful votes—which are represented in the legislature—to the unsuccessful vote—which is not represented, is thus shown graphically at a glance.

The total vote for members of the legislature in the city of New York at that election was 277,835 of which the Democrats cast 170,352 and elected *all* the members of the assembly. Although the Republicans had over 100,000 votes they had not a single representative in the assembly, senate or in the board of aldermen in the city.

Numberless other examples of the injustice of our present system of voting could be cited from elections in every part of the country.

As John Stuart Mill* has justly said, "democracy as hitherto practiced is the government of the whole people by a mere majority of the people exclusively represented.

"That the minority must yield to the majority, the smaller number to the greater, is a familiar idea; and accordingly, men think there is no necessity for using their minds any further, and it does not occur to them that there is any medium between allowing the smaller number to be equally powerful with the greater, and blotting out the smaller number altogether. In a representative body actually deliberating, the minority must of course be overruled; and in an equal democracy (since the opinions of the constituents, when they insist on them, determine those of the representative body), the majority of the people, through their representatives, will outvote and prevail over the

---

* "Considerations on Representative Goverument," American edition, p. 145.

22

Fig. 3.

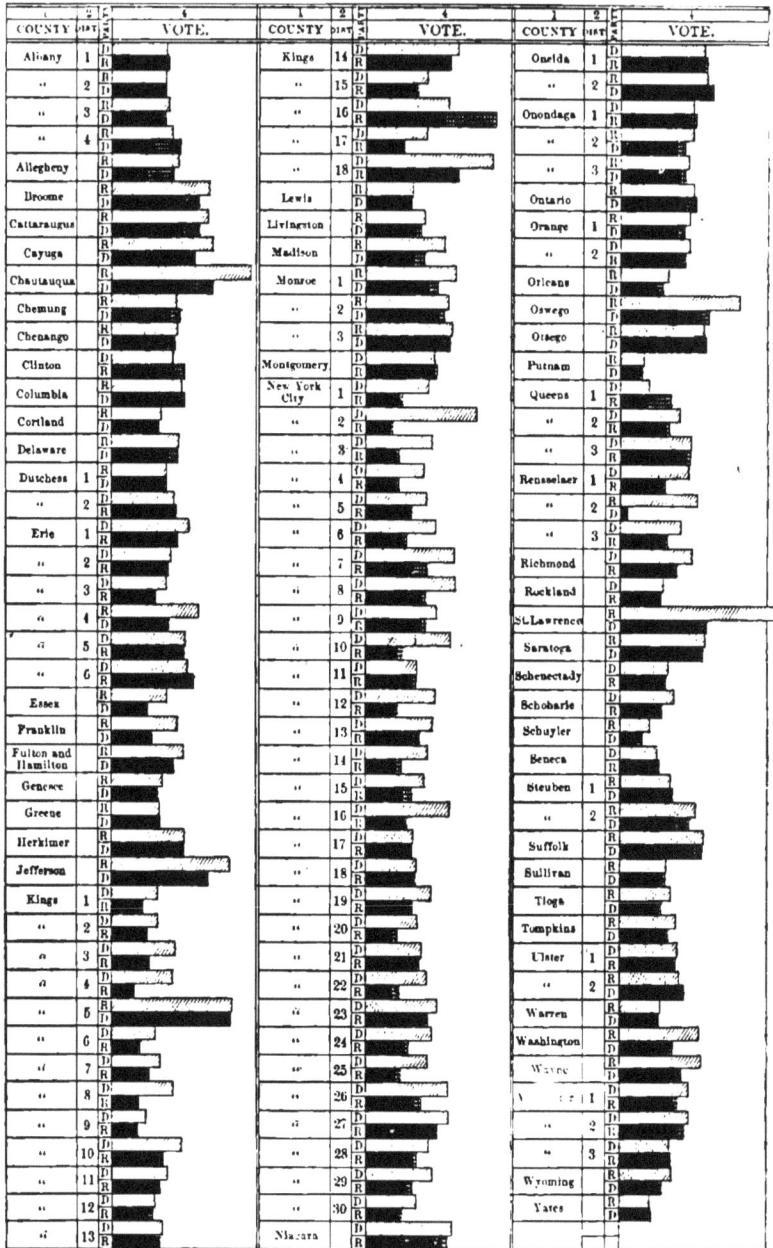

DIAGRAM SHOWING THE VOTE FOR ASSEMBLYMEN IN THE STATE OF NEW YORK IN 1892.

The areas shaded by diagonal lines represent the votes of the parties having a majority or plurality in the different districts; the black areas the votes of the minority parties and the small areas shaded with cross lines the scattering votes.

Fig. 4.   23

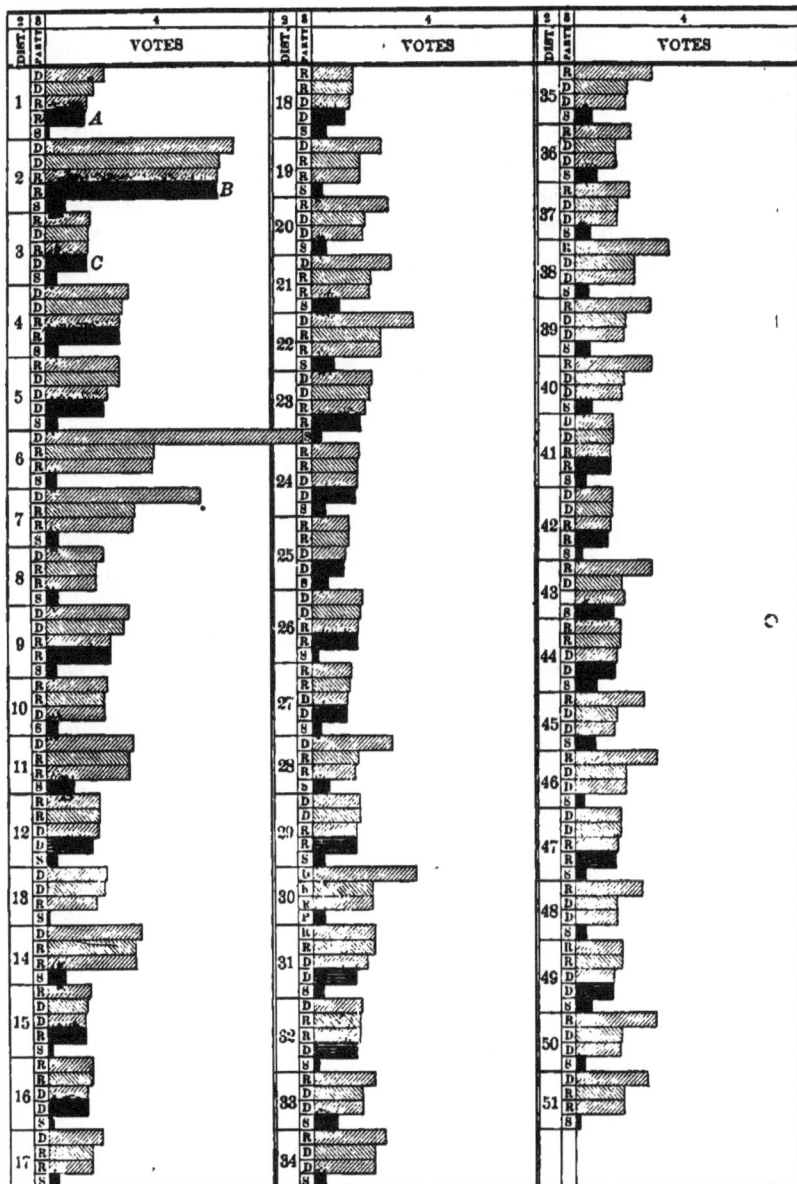

VOTE FOR MEMBERS OF HOUSE OF REPRESENTATIVES IN THE STATE OF ILLINOIS IN 1892.

In Illinois three Representatives are elected from each district and each voter can cast three votes for such representatives. He can distribute these as he likes; that is, he can give all of them to one candidate, or one and a half to one and one and a half to another, or one to each of three, and the three candidates in each district "highest in votes" are elected. In the above diagram the areas shaded with diagonal lines represent the votes for the three members who were elected in each of the different Districts. The areas shaded with horizontal lines represent the votes for candidates who were not elected, and the black areas the scattering votes.

minority and their representatives. But does it follow that the minority should have no representatives at all? Because the majority ought to prevail over the minority, must the majority have all the votes, the minority none? Is it necessary that the minority should not even be heard? Nothing but habit and old association can reconcile any reasonable being to the needless injustice. In a really equal democracy, every or any section would be represented, not disproportionately, but proportionately. A majority of the electors would always have a majority of the representatives; but a minority of the electors would always have a minority of the representatives. Man for man, they would be as fully represented as the majority. Unless they are, there is not equal government of inequality and privilege : one part of the people rule over the rest : there is a part whose fair and equal share of influence in the representation is withheld from them, contrary to all just government, but above all, contrary to the principle of democracy, which professes equality as its very root and foundation."

There is no other political maxim more firmly fixed in the minds of Americans and more implicitly believed in than " majorities should rule," and yet it often happens, as it did in Seneca and in other counties of New York in 1892, that a minority elects and the majority are unrepresented. The same thing occurred in the 1st and 4th districts in Albany, in Chemung, Clinton, Columbus, the 2d district of Dutchess, the 6th of Erie, Greene, the 16th district of Kings, Montgomery, both districts of Oneida, 1st of Onondaga, Ontario, Otsego, 1st district of Queens, 1st district of Steuben, 2d district of Ulster, 3d of Westchester and in Yates counties. It is true that the representatives in the State of New York were elected by the aggregate majority of the voters, but the black areas in the diagram show at a glance how large a proportion of the votes in the State of New York were unrepresented in the assembly after the election of 1892.

It must be remembered that the unrepresented were voiceless and voteless in the assembly. Consequently the powers of government were exercised by a majority *of the members elected.* These may and often do represent the views and interests of only a minority of the voters, so that democracy as it is now constituted often fails to accomplish its ostensible purpose. To quote again from Mill :

" All principles are most effectually tested by extreme cases. Suppose, then, that in a country governed by equal and universal suffrage, there is a contested election in every constituency, and every election is caused by a small majority. The parliament thus brought together represents little more than a bare majority of the people. This parliament proceeds to legislate, and adopts important measures by a ' bare majority of itself. What guarantee is there that these measures accord with the wishes of a majority of the people ? Nearly half the electors, having been outvoted at the hustings, have had no influence at all in the decision ; and the whole of them may be, a majority of them probably are, hostile to the measure, having voted against those by whom they have been carried. Of the remaining electors, nearly half have chosen representatives who, by supposition, have voted against the measures. It is possible, therefore, and even probable, that the opinion which has prevailed was agreeable only to a minority of the nation, though a majority of that portion of it whom the institutions of the country have erected into a ruling class. If democracy means the certain ascendancy of the majority, there are no means of insuring that, but by allowing every individual figure to tell equally in the summing up.''

The principle that the majority of the qualified voters should rule is not questioned. If all of them were represented in proportion to their numbers, then a majority of the representatives *would* rule and they would represent a majority of the qualified voters. Under existing conditions the majorities in our governing bodies often do not represent majorities of voters.

In his book on Proportional Representation the late Hon. Charles R. Buckalew of Pennsylvania said :

" It may be assumed that the average rate of virtual disfranchisement of voters in our contested popular elections is fully two-fifths of the total vote. This startling fact is the first one to be considered, and considered attentively, in any intelligent examination of the great subject of electoral reform in the United States ; for all schemes for the amendment of popular representation in government must be insufficient and illusory, which ignore it or underrate its enormous significance. For it means that popular elections are unjust ; it exposes the principal causes of their corruption, and it may instruct us, if we duly consider it, concerning those measures of change which will most certainly impart health, vigor and endurance to our political institutions."

At present a majority in any district, although it be a majority of only one vote may determine who shall represent the people in that district.   When parties are of about equal strength, as is nearly always the case in ordinary times in free republics, the really influential vote is not that of the mass of the citizens of one or the other party, but of a small faction, the "balance of power party" as it is sometimes called.   In a very forcible article in the *Nineteenth Century* for February, 1884, Mr. Robert H. Hayward calls attention to the baneful consequences of this instability of the representation caused by the shifting of small majorities in nearly balanced constituencies.   He says :

"If the beam of a balance be supported at a point very near to its centre of gravity, the shifting of a small weight determines its inclination to this side or that.   The system of majority voting has an analogous action ; it balances those of the electors who have serious political convictions and hold them strongly—the steady Liberals against the staunch Conservatives ; and then, if their weights are nearly equal, the inclination of the beam of the political balance is entirely at the mercy of a small body of electors, whose political views are determined at best by some ephemeral cry, some clever catchword, some panic fear, or some class interest, or in too many cases by those baser considerations which it may be hoped the Corrupt Practices Act of last session will have done something to restrain."

This condition has been jocosely designated as the "Scales of Injustice" and has been represented by the following engraving* in

THE SCALES OF INJUSTICE.

* "Proportional Representation," By Alfred Cridge, San Francisco.

which the "Balance of Power" is supposed to be adjusteu by the "influence" of the "floating vote." In other words, elections in districts, counties, cities, states, and even in the whole nation are at times, and perhaps not seldom, decided by the most corrupt portion of the voters in the community. Our municipal, state and national government then become illustrations of the Sovereignty of Bribery, Spoils and Patronage. As an English writer has said * "the tyranny of the majority is a sufficiently serious matter ; but the tyranny of a comparatively few variable, not to say venal, votes, is an unmitigated evil."

The same author says still further in commenting on our institutions :

"That government by a chance, or manipulated, majority of a part of the people should not only claim to be popular in the true sense, but should, practically, be recognized as such, tacitly, if not avowedly, would seem to be an unavoidable consequence of American democratic institutions. Whether unavoidable in fact, or, possibly, only an accident, such is the actual position of affairs."

Going on still further this writer says in explanation of this condition of things :

"But, surely, if the right of suffrage be the mark of sovereignty, and that sovereignty be the prerogative of the people, then those who possess the right also possess the sovereignty, and those to whom the prerogative belongs must be the people. If the logic is faulty, the conclusion remains true ; since the voters are, in the United States, to all intents and purposes the people. That is to say, that their will as expressed by their votes constitutes what is called popular government."

The real difficulty is that under our present system the will of the people does *not* secure full expression through their votes. Unpalatable as it may be, many of us cannot help recognizing the truth in the following picture of our institutions, which has been drawn by this same writer :

"This, then," he says, "seems to be, under present conditions,

---

* F. W. Grey, *Westminster Review.*

the *ultima ratio* of American Popular Government. *The People* is a
term equivalent to the majority of the votes for the time being; that
majority, from the nature of the case, since the masses greatly outnumber the classes, must, in only too many instances, consist of those least
fitted to exercise the right of suffrage. They hold, at any time, and
under all circumstances, the balance of power, their interest, in any
given election, being confined to the strongest of all possible motives
—self-interest. Moreover, being exploited by the professsional politicians, whose long and varied experience has taught them the full
value and utmost possibilities of such material, they are better organized than any other of the many elements that constitute the sovereign
people. That the professional politician, with unlimited money, perfect machinery, long training, and a sufficient supply of venal votes,
should be master of the situation—' boss the whole show '—is only the
natural effect of the adequate cause.''

This incisive critic points out too that Government of the People,
by the People, and for the People has often come to mean Government
of the Politicians, by the Politicians, and for the Politicians—and for
their privileged employés. He leaves the question whether these
evils be inseparable from democratic institutions or only accidents due
to local causes unanswered. It is though a very serious one to all
American citizens. To believe that these evils are inseparable from
our institutions is to despair of reform or improvement in our government.   '   .. ..'

In the phraseology of Guizot—'' the grand concern of society is that
the power of reason, justice and truth, which is dispersed among the
individuals who compose society, should be collected from all sides and
concentrated into one focus and called to the occupation of power and
be organized into an actual government,'' and—as that distinguished
author says—'' what we call *representation* is nothing else than a means
to arrive at this result, it is   *   *   *   but a natural process by
which public reason, which alone has a right to govern society, may
be extracted from the bosom of society itself.''

CHAPTER III.

And now as a writer in the *Nineteenth Century* * asks—"what does majority representation mean? It means"—he answers—"that the majority shall have everything and the minority nothing. It means that, whether the number of members to be elected by each constituency be large or small, the whole of the representation shall be monopolized by that party which polls one more than half the votes and that party which polls one less than half the votes shall have no representation at all."

Going back to the history of the evolution of civil liberty and what do we find—always that good government is a sequence to a fair and just representation of the people in the administration of public affairs and the exercise of political power. Our misgovernment comes from the fact that the people who are adjudged qualified to take part in governmental affairs are not fairly represented. In the city of New York every voter at elections must practically choose between two candidates in voting for aldermen, members of the legislature or members of Congress. He has no choice of nominees excepting for those whom the politicians choose to give him. If the majority in his district is against him he is left without a representative. This condition of things is not peculiar to New York City or New York State but exists nearly everywhere, and grows out of the system of electing, by a majority of votes, single representatives from districts in cities, counties and states. This condition of public affairs was described with great clearness and force in the article on The Machinery of Politics and Proportional Representation,† from which quotations have already been made, and in which it is said:

---

* "Proportional *vs.* Majority Representation." By Albert Grey, M. P., in the *Nineteenth Century* for December, 1884.

† This appeared in the *American Law Review* for January, 1872. The authorship is not known to the writer.

"The unsatisfactory symptoms are everywhere much the same. The character of the political machinery everywhere in use is such that a great amount of preliminary work is needed to set it a going,— caucusing and canvassing, pulling of wires and greasing of wheels,— a work that from its nature must needs be performed by a small knot of experienced workmen. It is inevitable that in this state of things there should arise political ' rings,' small coteries of political managers with every opportunity to control and direct the course of party politics to their mutual advantage. Their injurious influence is felt both by the public man and by the private citizen. Public life as a career becomes practically closed to men of marked character and independent views. The private citizen feels himself to be a tool in the hands of his political advisers, and, finding the more obscure and irksome of his public duties—the attendance upon primary and nominating caucuses—not only distasteful, but futile, abandons them in disgust. Nor does he find more satisfaction in the exercise of the suffrage itself. Though nominally free to vote for whom he pleases, the knowledge that his vote is thrown away unless it is given for the regular candidates, that is, that he may as well not vote at all as not obey his political advisers, binds him hand and foot. He finds himself practically obliged to choose among candidates for none of whom he probably cares a farthing, so that indifference to his more public duties follows fast upon his distaste for the more obscure. He soon cares as little to go to the polls as to go to the caucus. And indeed he has everything to foster this indifference, for he knows that if he belongs to the majority party his vote will probably not be needed ; if to the other, that it will be of no avail.

"But if the preliminaries of an election are thus injurious and demoralizing both to public and private citizens, the results of an election are a positive injustice. Our elections fail in their chief purpose,—that of furnishing a fairly representative body. It would seem that a deliberative assembly, standing in the place of the whole body of citizens, to discuss and decide in their behalf all matters of public moment, should as nearly as possible resemble in its composition the political community for which it stands, and that whatever varieties of interest and opinion exist in the constituency should find adequate expression among their representatives. The ideal method of elections is certainly the one that would thus make the elected body a perfect epitome of the body politic, giving to every political party large or small, its fair share of members in the proportion of its numerical strength. The fair and just system of representation would be a system of proportional representation.

" How far the present system of voting is from producing any such results, and how unjustly and unfairly it works, is notorious. A political contest is a struggle, not for a fair share of the representation, but for the whole. The outvoted electors are reduced to political slavery ; they have no voice whatever in public affairs. Their rights of representation are taken from them, and are appropriated by their conquerors. It is a war without quarter, and it is a contest in which the sacrifices of the victors are hardly less serious than the losses of the defeated party. Everything has to be yielded for the sake of victory, and as eligibility becomes necessarily the prime quality in a candidate, it naturally follows that, as we have said, men of mark give place to men of no mark, and the representative assembly comes to be composed for the most part of second-rate men, mere standard-bearers in party warfare, hardly better known or more acceptable to the men who voted for them than to their opponents.

" These evils,—the disfranchisement of minorities and the consequent tyranny of majorities ; the tyranny of political managers over their followers, and the consequent helplessness and indifference of the electors ; the tyranny of these same managers over public men, and the consequent withdrawal from public life of men who are seeking an honorable and independent career,—these evils are co-extensive with representative institutions, and are mainly attributed, by those publicists who have undertaken to trace their causes, to the natural working of an objectionable electoral machinery. The scheme of majority voting, as almost everywhere practised, is not only vicious in principle, since it excludes from representation a large fraction of the electors, but it is so crude and defective in its operations that it needs, as we have said, a special force of trained engineers to make it work at all. It is natural that these men should make it work to suit themselves."

In another article on Proportional Representation, published in

Putnam's Magazine as long ago as June, 1870, the writer described the evils of our present system of representation in the following words :

" Our practice contravenes the fundamental principle of republican government, which is that the majority must rule. This principle is essential to the idea of such government. When the power resides in all the citizens, the voice of the greater number must prevail, or the minority will rule. This principle, carried to its legitimate result, requires that every question shall be decided by the majority of those in whom resides the ultimate power. As all citizens are equal in rights, the consent of the larger number must necessarily overbear the consent of the smaller number. * * * If the electoral machinery is such as to express only the choice of a majority of the city's voters, the minority is lost. In other words, all the persons concerned in a question and having the right to decide it should be heard in person or by representation.

*   *   *   *   *

" Under the false pretences of party, the elector is cheated or seduced into voting for one of two men, neither of whom he likes or would trust in the management of his private affairs. He is reduced to a choice of evils, and he makes it under the pressure of party discipline. We all know that it is the custom for two conventions, supposing, as is generally the case, the division of the electors into two parties, to select each a candidate, and for the voter to choose between the two, or lose his vote altogether. This is the system in its best estate, which supposes the primary meetings to contain only voters of the party, and the delegates to be fairly chosen, and these in their turn to discharge fairly their own duties of nominating candidates. * * * But since there is no legal or adequate provision for the regulation of primary assemblies or nominating conventions, they are in other districts carried by fraud or violence, so that it may be said of not a few that the scheme then established is for two bodies of incompetent or ill-intentioned men to put up each a man, and for the rest of the community to take their choice between the two.

*   *   *   *   *

"A choice of bad men is, however not the only evil of the system.

The good men who find their way into our legislatures are crippled by it. Their influence is weakened and their independence menaced. When one of them opposes a favorite scheme of the party managers of his district, he is sure to receive warning as well as a remonstrance. Thus the representative and the constitutent are both demoralized.

"These evils do not spring from a corrupt community. The majority of the people are not debauched. The fault lies in a vicious electoral system, which produces a representation neither of parties nor of the general public, which constrains the majority, and stifles the voices of large portions of the people.

"The importance of representation, or rather the evil of nonrepresentation, is measured by the value of popular government. By leaving a large number of citizens without voice in the state, we not only lose the benefit of their counsel and coöperation, but we make them discontented. The fraud and falsehood of the system beget other frauds and falsehoods, and lower the moral tone of the whole community. The vast power and patronage of government often depend upon a few votes. Need we wonder that force and fraud should both be used to procure them ? Parties are themselves deceived by their preponderance in legislatures, without considering how far it rests upon a like preponderance out of doors. The opinions and wishes of large portions of the people are disregarded. They see measures of great significance adopted which they disapprove, but are powerless to prevent, while they are unable to procure a consideration of others which they think indispensable to the general good. If we can devise a remedy, if we can by any means procure an electoral system, by which the wishes of the whole people will be made known, and the votes of their real representatives taken, on all measures of legislation, we shall have saved the state from the danger which seems now to be impending over it."

The objections to elections by a majority were also presented very clearly in an article by Mr. Leonard Courtney, published in the Nineteenth Century of July, 1879.

These he said are that : "You cannot trust any exclusive party to act with justice to those who are wholly in their power, and whose cause cannot be pleaded before them. If the minority have not some one to speak up for their feelings and desires, the majority will act with injustice towards them ; and this not so much from any set purpose to be unjust as from the natural incapacity of men to understand the wrongs of their neighbors. This is the case whether we consider the action of employers towards workmen or of workmen towards employers ; of men towards women ; and, if women were the rulers to the exclusion of men, no doubt it would be very much the same of women towards men. No party can be trusted to exercise justice to an excluded party. No one possesses the intelligence and imagination necessary before he can put himself in the position of another so as to understand what another wants. As the old proverb says, ' No one knows how the shoe pinches except him who wears it.' A man who wore sandals could not very well understand the wants of the man who wore shoes. There would, again, be no living connection between the ruling body and the excluded body. There is no connection between the excluded minority and the ruling majority. If men obtain no share in the representation which constitutes the authority of a country, their po-litical energies die away and disappear. They have faculties and political feelings, but they assume a rudimentary character, they become unenergetic, and so their energies entirely pass away.''

The same writer described the effect of the present system on can-didates by saying :

'' Under the old plan the primary object is generally this : ' We must have a man to keep the party together. We want a man who will not lose the support of any section of the party.' This last was the great point held in view. You must keep the party together ; therefore your candidate must have in him nothing that will drive away any members of the party from adhering to the choice of the few. In order to do that you must have a man who will offend no-body—who will be far from all tendency to kick over the traces ; · whether in thought or in action, he must keep well within the party lines. If he will vote steadily and pledge himself to support the leader for the time being, he has the best chance of success. That is the way in which the mass of members have been chosen, and candidates have always been obliged to bear this in mind. The first duty of a candi-date is to be prudent—not to offend anybody—to subdue his mind as far as possible to the lowest level compatible with any life at all, and to be careful not to disturb the prejudices of any section at all. That is the necessity of getting a majority of any constituency. The result is to produce a candidate with the gift of mediocrity. You would not find a majority of your constituency to go together for a man who is pronounced in his opinions, or in his character, or in the force of his thought; and the result is, that the strongest man has to be put aside in order that the moderate man may be run, because the moderate man has the best chance of winning. If this is anything like an accurate representation of the facts, the result must be a degradation of the character of your candidates, and of your electoral body. If you get indifferent materials to work with, you cannot do good work; and if you send into the legislature such men as I have described, you will not make a brilliant assembly out of them."

This picture is as true of practical politics in this country as it is of the condition of public affairs in England which it was intended to describe. An American writer has pointed out that in· this country the voter: "Though nominally free to vote for whom he pleases, the knowledge that his vote is thrown away unless it is given for the regular candidates binds him hand and foot. He finds himself obliged to choose among candidates for none of whom he probably cares a farthing, so that indifference to his more important public duties follows fast his distaste for the more obscure (*i. e.*, attendance at primary meetings and nominating caucuses). He soon cares as little to go to the poll as to go to the caucus, and thus the political energies of large sections of the community are condemned to atrophy and extinction, for, unless men know that their vote can be made effectual, the right to vote is not appreciated, and the so-called privilege of citizenship assumes in their opinion the appearance of a bitter mockery."

These evils are so great and are so apparent that many who have the true interests of their country, their state and locality very much at heart often feel and speak bitterly and in a more or less despairing tone of the future. Thus Mr. Simon Sterne in his book on Representative Government says:

"The process of creating a majority demoralizes most of those who compose it; it demoralizes them in this sense, that it excludes the action of their higher moral attributes, and brings into operation the lower motives. They are compelled to disregard all individuality and therefore all genuine earnestness of opinion ; to discard their political knowledge ; their deliberate judgment ; their calm and conscientious reflection, all must be withdrawn, or brought down to a conformity with those who possess the least of these qualities. * * * Wherever the majority is not held in check by a minority of almost equal strength, it becomes a despotism and a despotism not founded on the sentiments or traditions of a people can only perpetuate and consolidate its power by intrigue and fraud."

Mr. Buckalew in a speech made in Philadelphia in 1869 said :

"Look at your existing political action and see whether it is not a struggle for power instead of a struggle for justice ; whether it is not a struggle by each interest to obtain all it can and retain all it can, and to keep away from an opposing interest anything like a fair distribution of power or fair treatment."

That despair often takes the place of discouragement we all know and perhaps sometimes feel, and when we hear of men as distinguished as Dr. A. P. Peabody saying in a Baccalaureate Sermon at Harvard, that "instead of a government by the people, we are threatened, if the threat be not already fulfilled, with an oligarchy of demagogues, for which a decent constitutional monarchy would be welcome,"—we feel that there may be reason for anxiety for the future if not for despair. Perhaps few of us have yet descended to the depths from which Herbert Spencer has so recently renounced his faith in free institutions, which, he says, "originally was strong (though always joined with the belief that the maintenance and success of them is a question of popular character), has in these later years been greatly decreased by the conviction that the fit character is not possessed by any people, nor is likely to be possessed for ages to come. A nation of which the legislators vote as they are bid, and of which the workers surrender their rights of selling their labor as they please, has neither the ideas nor the sentiments needed for the maintenance of liberty. Lacking them, we are on the way back to the rule of the strong hand in the shape of the bureaucratic despotism of a socialistic organization, and then of a military despotism which must follow it ; if, indeed, some social crash does not bring this last upon us more quickly."

Matthew Arnold says : " Sages and saints are apt to be severe, it is true ; apt to take a gloomy view of the society in which they live, and to prognosticate evil of it. But then it must be added that their prognostications are very apt to turn out right. Plato's account of the most gifted and brilliant community of the ancient world, of that Athens of his to which we all owe so much, is despondent enough. ' There is but a very small remnant,' he says, ' of honest followers of wisdom * * * who have tasted how sweet and blessed a possession is wisdom, and who can fully see, moreover, the madness of the multitude, and that there is no one, we may say, whose action in public matters is sound.'

" Perhaps you will say," Mr. Arnold continues, " that the majority is sometimes good ; that its impulses are good generally, and its action is good occasionally. But it lacks principle, it lacks persistence ; if to-day its good impulses prevail, they succumb to-morrow ; sometimes it goes right, but it is very apt to go wrong. Even a popular orator, or a popular journalist, will hardly say that the multitude may be trusted to have its judgment generally just, and its action generally virtuous. It may be better, it is better, that the body of the people, with all its faults, should act for itself, and control its own affairs. * * * But still, the world being what it is, we must surely expect the aims and doings of the majority of men to be at present very faulty, and this in a numerous community no less than in a small one. * * * Admit that for the world, as we hitherto know it, what the philosophers and prophets say is true : that the majority are unsound. Even in nations with exceptional gifts, even in the Jewish state, the Athenian state, the majority are unsound. But there is the *remnant*. Now the important thing as regards states such as Judah and Athens, is not that the remnant bears but a small proportion to the majority : the great thing for states like Judah and Athens is, that the remnant must in positive bulk be so small, and therefore so powerless for reform. To be a voice outside the state, speaking to mankind or to the future, perhaps shaking the actual state to pieces in doing so, one man will suffice. To reform the state in order to save it, to preserve it by changing it, a body of workers is needed as well as a leader —a considerable body of workers, placed at many points and operating in many directions. * * * In our great modern states, where the scale of things is so large, it does seem as if the remnant might be so increased as to become an actual power, even though the majority be unsound. Then the lover of wisdom may come out from under his wall, the lover of goodness will not be alone among the wild beasts. To enable the remnant to succeed, a large strengthening of its numbers is everything.''

One of the main objects of the reform which is advocated in this volume and which has been variously designated as minority representation, proportional representation and personal representation is to give what Matthew Arnold calls '' the righteous remnant'' or the minority a chance to succeed and to exercise its due influence and power. It, of course, would be optimistic to assume that minorities are always righteous but it would be safe to assert, and be quite true, that the righteous remnant is always a minority. What is proposed and intended by minority representation is to give to each minority a share of the members in the representative body proportional to its share in the electoral body, along with such influence as it may be able to obtain by the opportunity for statement and discussion of its opinions in the legislative assembly. This ought not to be confounded, as it very often is, with government by a minority. Its purpose and effect would be to give a more perfect representation to every considerable and influential body of opinion in the whole electorate, and thus a more perfect representation of *all*, and therefore of the real majority. Such representation would include the '' righteous remnants.'' It would give us a system under which the electors *as a whole*, and not merely a majority, would be represented ; under which minorities would always have a hearing, while the majority would be sure of their just preponderance.

In this view of the case some reformers believe that a better method of electing representatives for our national, state and municipal governing bodies may be, and in fact has been, found and adopted and which will be explained.

It has been pointed out, and most voters have had occasion to experience, that they have little or absolutely no power of choice in the selection of candidates who are chosen. These—to use the vernacular of the practical politicians—are "fixed" by the managers of the political primary meetings and organizations in which the independent voter generally can have little or no voice. In voting he must nearly always accept one of two candidates in the nomination of neither of whom has he had any influence. If he votes with the minority he is —at any rate so far as his opinions and interests differ from those of the opposing party and its candidate—unrepresented.

That such a system should fail "to call to the occupation of power the scattered and incomplete fragments of reason, justice and truth— or "the righteous remnants" which exist in society ought perhaps not to surprise us. Instead of government of and for the People by those who are qualified it has given us in too many cases government of all the People for and by Political "Bosses." *Free*, FULL, and JUST representation of the people, qualified to exercise political power, is the fundamental principle on which all just republican government is dependent and it is by the adoption of this principle that liberty has always been achieved and maintained.

There is abundant evidence to show that under our existing system representation is not *Free*, nor FULL, nor JUST. How can we secure more liberty in the choice of our representatives, how can we have our own views and interests more completely represented, how can we have fair play in elections?

CHAPTER IV.

THE REPRESENTATION OF MINORITIES.

Those who have seen and felt the injustice and the evils of our present method of electing representatives have proposed various expedients by which the evil may be, in a greater or lesser degree, mitigated. These schemes all have the one feature in common, that of uniting or grouping neighboring districts together *and electing more than one representative from each of the consolidated districts.* It should be clearly understood that such an enlargement of districts by consolidating a number of small ones, does not imply an increase in the total number of representatives to be elected. It only means that instead of electing one representative in each of say three small districts that these districts shall be united so as to form one larger one, and the three members will then all be elected from it, and each voter will be given the privilege of voting for any or all of these different candidates. The plan contemplates the consolidation of small districts into larger ones, and apportioning the present number of representatives among the enlarged districts.

Some method is then provided by which the voter can either vote for a number of candidates or can concentrate his voting power on one or two.

To make this quite clear it may be explained that in the State of New York, and most other states, only one member of the legislature is elected from each district. Usually there are then only two candidates in each district, one Republican the other a Democrat, and often neither of them fit men for the office, and not infrequently both disreputable. Notwithstanding this the voter has no other choice—he must vote for either one or the other or lose his vote.

In the State of Illinois, to provide, in a measure, against these evils what is called "cumulative voting" has been adopted. Under this system the districts have been so formed that *three* members of the

House of Representatives are elected from each district and the constitution of that state provides that *"each voter may cast as many votes for one candidate as there are representatives to be elected, or may distribute the same, or equal parts thereof, among the candidates as he shall see fit, and the candidates highest in votes shall be declared elected."* In other words a voter may cast three votes for one candidate, or one and a half for one and one and a half for another, or one each for three candidates. Representing three candidates by letters and the votes by numerals, they may be given in any of the three following ways :

A—3 votes	A—1½ votes	A—1 vote
	B—1½ "	B—1 "
		C—1 "

These votes may, of course, be given to any candidates the voter may select. To show the working of this, it will be assumed that in some district of Illinois there are 9680 Democratic and 4920 Republican voters. Having estimated their numbers before the election, the Democrats knowing that they had a majority would nominate two candidates and each Democratic voter could cast 1½ votes for each candidate. They would then each receive 14,520 votes. The Republicans being in a minority would nominate only one, and they would each cast three votes, or "plump" for him, as it is called, so that he would receive 14,760 votes. It will thus be seen that both parties in this district were represented, the Democrats being in a majority elect two candidates and the Republicans one.

The party having a bare majority can always, under this system, elect two candidates, and if the minority have more than a fourth as many votes as their antagonists they can elect one member. This system thus gives not only a representation to both parties, under the conditions named, but it also gives much greater freedom to the voters than the old system of electing single members from the different districts does, and it has therefore been very properly called by its chief advocate, the late Senator Charles R. Buckalew, *free voting.* Its freedom consists in this, that the voter can vote for any one or all of three candidates, any or all of whom may be elected. Under the ordinary system only one candidate can be elected in a district.

Next, if the voter has a preference for any candidate over others, he can give all his votes for the one, for two, or for three if he chooses. It thus facilitates independent voting. If unfit candidates are nominated, it gives very much greater opportunities of success to a revolting, bolting or independent party, because the bolters can concentrate their votes on one candidate. As has been explained, any candidate may be elected if he gets all the votes of *more* than a fourth of the voters. That is, by uniting a fourth of the voters + 1 in any district, they can always elect a representative of their own. Thus in most of the districts in southern Illinois, the Democrats have large majorities. Under the ordinary system, of electing single representatives from each district, the Republicans in that part of the state would not be represented, but under the method of cumulative or "*free*" voting, which has been established in that state, if the Republicans in any district have more than a fourth of the voters, they can elect a representative. In the northern part of Illinois the reverse condition of things exists. There the Republicans predominate, and if there was no freedom of voting, most of the Democrats from that section would be unrepresented.

The system of free voting thus gives both parties a representation proportionate to their numbers. It has the advantage that *it gives a number of voters much smaller than a majority the power to elect their own representative.* In most sections of the country the labor party has no representatives, for the reason that there are comparatively few or no districts in which they have a majority of the votes. Under the system of free voting which prevails in Illinois, if the party can control more than a fourth of the votes in any district they could elect a candidate. The same is true of any other class of people. If those who are most intelligent, who have been industrious, frugal and prudent, and who have consequently accumulated property, and who pay the taxes, fear God and love righteousness, desire a representative it is within their power to elect one if they unite, and if they can control the requisite fourth of the votes plus one or more. In other words, it gives any class of voters exceeding one-fourth of all in any district, the power of electing their own representative.

CHAPTER V.

The system of cumulative or " free " *voting* which has been described was adopted in the constitution of the State of Illinois in 1870 and has been in use ever since 1872. There has therefore been abundant opportunity of ascertaining its merits and demerits from practical experience. In order to get the testimony of persons in different parts of that state who have had opportunities of observing the working and the results of this system, a circular of inquiry was prepared by the writer and sent to persons interested in public affairs in different parts of Illinois. The following is a copy of that circular :

NEW YORK, November 25, 1893.

DEAR SIR :

A Convention has been called and delegates have been chosen at the recent election in the State of New York for the revision of its constitution. In view of this a number of persons in the city of New York are considering the advisability of recommending the adoption of provisions for some form of cumulative voting, for the election of members of our municipal and state legislative bodies, similar to the system by which the members of the House of Representatives in the State of Illinois are now elected. Under it, as you are doubtless aware, three representatives are elected from each district and each voter may cast as many votes for them as there are representatives to be elected, which he may distribute as he likes. Some of the persons here who are interested in this subject desire very much to get information with reference to the practical working of cumulative voting in your state, and it is with that object in view that this circular is sent to you, and to others who have opportunities of judging of the merits and demerits of the system referred to. You will be doing a favor to some of the friends of good government and giving that cause valuable assistance by answering the following inquiries and giving any other information concerning the operation and effects of cumulative voting in your state, which may throw light on that subject.

1st. Does the system of cumulative voting which has been adopted in Illinois for the election of representatives to the legislature accomplish the object for which it was intended; that is, does it give the minority party in your district, whichever it may be, a representative in the legislature?

2d. What effect does it have on the nomination of candidates for office? In other words are better and more intelligent candidates nominated and elected than were chosen under the old system of electing one member from each district?

3d. Is there any practical difficulty in the operation of the system, either through the ignorance of voters, or of inspectors of election, in counting the votes or in any other way?

4th. Is there more or less opportunity under this than under the old system, for bribery and corruption, false or erroneous counting?

5th. It has been objected to this system that if a very popular man is nominated that an undue proportion of the votes in his district may be concentrated on him and that the remaining two candidates might thus be elected by a small minority—in your experience is this often or ever the case?

6th. Do you consider the system a fair and just one, to all parties concerned; does it promote good government, or is the old system now in use in all other states, of electing only one representative from each district and giving each voter only one vote to be preferred?

7th. Would it be advantageous to increase the size of the districts so as to elect five, seven or more representatives from each, and give the voter the privilege of casting as many votes as there are representatives to be elected, and cumulate them as he chooses?

8th. In your opinion would there be any advantage in adopting the cumulative system for the election of members of Congress or members of boards of aldermen in cities?

9th. Can you suggest any other system or method of electing representatives which in your judgment would secure the election of better men or improve legislation?

10th. The parties making the inquiries request that you will add below any further comments or suggestions as will aid them in getting full and correct information concerning the advantages and disadvantages of cumulative voting, as it has been adopted in your state.

· Sign here,

Name, _____

Address, _____

_____

Party Politics, _____

When replies to the above inquiries have been written enclose this circular and mail it in the envelope addressed to

M. N. FORNEY,

47 Cedar St., New York City.

Copies of this circular of inquiry were sent to the editors of papers in all parts of the State of Illinois, and additional copies were also enclosed in stamped blank envelopes with the request to the editor that he should address the envelopes to persons in his district who are interested in public affairs, and who would likely give intelligent replies to the inquiries. In all about 150 replies were received, which of course represented a wide range of opinion and of varying degrees of intelligence.

The answers to the first question :

Does the system of cumulative voting which has been adopted in Illinois for the election of representatives to the legislature accomplish the object for which it was intended; that is, does it give the minority party in your district, whichever it may be, a representative in the legislature ? were almost unanimous in the opinion that the system of cumulative voting *does* give the minority party representation. The following are a few of these answers received from Democrats, the residence of the respondent being given in italics :

" It does. In my judgment it is one of the best laws ever enacted, and prevents dangerous majorities. Minorities always are represented." Dem. *Mattoon.*

" Yes. And in every other district in the state, thus distributing party representation throughout the state, instead of consolidating the respective party representation in localities." Dem. *Austin, Cook Co.*

" Yes. It meets all expectations. There have been but two or three instances in the whole State of Illinois since 1870, when the constitution was adopted where any district has had more than two of the three members of the House from the same party." Dem. *Charleston.*

" It does almost always. Sometimes the minority is so small that the dominant party in a district nominates and elects the entire number required, but this happens infrequently." Dem. *Chicago.*

" We are here in the 47th Senatoral District ; since the cumulative system of voting has been adopted the two leading parties (Democratic and Republican) have made it a practice to place only two candidates each in the field. The Democrats are in the majority but the Republicans never fail to secure one representative." Dem. *East St. Louis.*

"Yes, the majority party has found it impossible after several attempts to elect their candidates." Dem. *Chester.*

"Yes, except on extraordinary occasions." Dem. *Monmouth.*

"Yes, when the guess of the minority and the guess of the majority in nominating conventions are correct." Dem. *Chicago.*

"Yes, it gives one representative to the minority but sometimes at the expense of the majority which is traded or bought." Dem. *Flora.*

"It does. Still when the vote between the parties is very close each party having two candidates and three to be elected it results that some popular candidate draws from his running mate and the minority party elects two of the three representatives." Dem. *Carlyle.*

"Yes. We the Democrats always have our tickets printed 1½ votes for each candidate and always nominate just two candidates and elect them, only giving the Republicans one representative." Dem. *Carlyle, Clinton Co.*

"Yes. It has very seldom been attempted by any one party to elect *all* the representatives in a district and when tried it has failed." Dem. *Pontiac.*

"In my district the minority party as shown by the election of 1892 elected two representatives and the majority party but one. This was caused by the tidal wave of that year. The district when formed was largely Republican and the Democrats named but one man, hence the above result." Dem. *Evanston.*

"I can't say that it *fully* accomplishes the intended result. It gives the minority party one representative, and at one election the third party elected one man—only once though." Dem. *Havana.*

The following replies were received from Republicans:

"Yes, as a whole. The longer it is in force the better the people understand it and the smoother it works." Rep. *Collinsville.*

"It does fully, and has never failed I believe in giving the minority a representation." Rep. *Dixon.*

"In all districts where the minority party have one-third of the *votes* they seldom, or. never, fail to get one representative. I am in a part of the old 34th district. We Republicans never failed to get one member against an odds of 2000 majority." Rep. *Havana.*

".The minority in this district never has failed to elect a member under our present system of legislative voting. I never have known it to fail in any case in the state." Rep. *Champaign.*

" It does except in districts where the minority party has less than one fourth of the entire vote." Rep. *Ottawa.*

" It does. This district is so strongly Democratic that without it the Republicans could have no representative. As it is the Republicans always elect one of the three representatives, thus the minority of our district is heard." Rep. *Beardstown.*

" It does. In this district the Democrats are very much in the minority but by casting the three votes alone each voter (one for each representative) for their own nominee he is elected." Rep. *Elgin.*

" Yes; and by reason of the temptation to *plumping*—that is cumulating three votes on one canditate—it frequently enables the minority party to elect *two* of the three members." Rep. *Chicago.*

" Yes. It always gives the minority one and sometimes two. All accidents result in favor of the minority, which not infrequently elects two members because of an unequal division of the majority vote between two candidates." Rep. *Springfield.*

" Under the cumulative system the minority party has always had a representative, and sometimes two, when there was more ' plumping ' on one side than on the other." Rep. *Warsaw.*

" It does. Sometimes, though rarely, it gives a third and weaker party a representative instead of the party second in strength." Rep. *Bushnell.*

" Yes, invariably. The Republicans might elect three, if every voter cast one vote straight for each candidate, but they always concede one candidate to the opposite party for prudential reasons." Rep. *Naperville.*

" It does, and may give two if the stronger party do not put up good men." Rep. *Beardstown.*

" Yes, it does in every district in the state. At the first election held under the law there was one district so strong Republican that they elected all three representatives." Rep. *Effingham.*

To show from the election returns what effect this system has
on an election in the whole state and to compare the results with those
in the State of New York the returns of the election of members of the
legislature in 1892 in Illinois have been plotted in a diagram, Fig.
4, p. 23, which is similar to Fig. 3, which represents the vote in
the State of New York, in the same year. Inasmuch as each voter
in Illinois has three votes, the votes cast for each candidate have been
divided by three in order that the diagram may be comparable with
Fig. 3, which represents the results of the New York election.

. Before comparing the two diagrams a little further explanation is
needed. In those districts in Illinois in which the two prominent parties
are nearly equal, it happens often that each is sanguine enough to think
that they can elect *two* candidates to the House of Representatives, and
consequently they each put two in the field. As only three can be
elected of course one of the four must be defeated. This was the case
in the 1st, 2d, 3d, 4th, and 5th districts. In each of the first two,
two Democrats were elected and one Republican, and in the third two
Republicans and one Democrat. In the 1st and 2d districts a Republican was defeated in each, and in the third a Democrat. Now in the
first two it cannot be said that the Republicans were not represented.
They had one member for each district, but were not fully represented
according to their numbers. This is also true of the Democrats in the
3d district. The areas *A*, *B*, and *C*, Fig. 4, which represent the
votes cast for the unsuccessful candidates, are therefore shaded with
dark horizontal lines, and show the voters who were only partially
represented. The small black areas represent the scattering voters
who cast their votes for Prohibition, Populist and Labor party candidates, none of whom were elected.

A comparison of the two diagrams, Figs. 3 and 4, the one representing the vote in the State of New York under the old system of
single representatives from each district, and the other that in Illinois
under free voting, shows very distinctly the relative number of voters
who are unrepresented in the two states—the black areas in both cases
indicating the unrepresented, or practically disfranchised, and the dark
areas in Fig. 4 those who were only partially represented. By comparing these two diagrams, the black areas show at a glance how very

much greater the number of unrepresented voters was in the State of New York, under our present system of electing one representative from each district, than it was in Illinois when three representatives are elected by a system of free voting.

The observations of John Stuart Mill again serve our purpose best in commenting on the kind of injustice which the diagram shows, resulted from the election in New York. The only answer he says "which can possibly be made is, that as different opinions predominate in different localities, the opinion which is in a minority in some places has a majority in others; and, on the whole, every opinion which exists in the constituencies obtains its fair share of voices in the representation. * * * The constituencies to which most of the highly educated and public-spirited persons in the country belong, those of the large towns, are now in great part either unrepresented or misrepresented. The electors who are on a different side in party politics from the local majority are mis-represented. Of those who are on the same side, a large proportion are misrepresented, having been obliged to accept the man who had the greatest number of supporters in their political party, though his opinions may differ from theirs in every other point. * * * Speaking generally, the choice of the majority is determined by that portion of the body who are the most timid, the most narrow-minded and prejudiced, or who cling most tenaciously to the exclusive class interest."

In addition to what Mill has so forcibly said it may be added that it is but a slight satisfaction for a Republican merchant or banker in New York City, who is denied representation in the state legislature, to know that a rural member from St. Lawrence or Chemung county, who belongs to the same party, will vote to levy taxes or legislate on financial affairs for him; nor will a Democrat in Cattaraugus feel compensated for the defeat of his party in his own county, by the knowledge that his views and interests will be looked after at Albany, by a Tammany heeler from the slums of New York City. Under a system of free voting the Republican merchant or banker of New York could help to elect a member who would coincide with his views and opinions and who would understand and could and would represent his interests, and the Democratic farmer in Chautauqua could help to send some one to the assembly who was sound on the oleomargarine and other rural questions. *Free voting* permits minorities in all sections to be represented, and thus gives to every body of men who cannot appear in the legislature in person, the right claimed by Franklin, "to appear by an agent."

From the almost unanimous testimony of many witnesses in all parts of the states who replied to the circular which was sent to them, and who gave their answers quite independently of each other, and also from the returns of the state election in Illinois in 1892 which have been plotted in Fig. 4 it is shown conclusively that the system of cumulative or free voting which has been adopted in that state, *does* give the minority party, in every district in which it has more than a fourth of the votes, a representative in the legislature. As a matter of fact there was not a single district in Illinois in 1892 in which one party elected all three of the representatives, although that might and has happened when the minority party had less than a fourth of all the votes in some districts.

Whatever may be thought of the cumulative system it must be conceded that through it *minorities are represented*. Is this a desirable result or is it not?

In a report to the U. S. Senate made on March 2, 1869, Mr. Buckalew from the Select Committee on Representative Reform said :

" By the free vote the whole mass of electors are brought into direct relations with government, and particularly with that department or branch of government which makes the laws. All will participate really in choosing representatives, and all will be represented in fact. Now, the beaten body of electors *choose nothing, unless it be mortification*, and are not represented at all. For the theory that they are represented by the successful candidates against whom they have voted— that these candidates when installed in office represent them—is plainly false. An elected official represents the opinions and the will of those who choose him, and not of those who oppose his selection. As to the latter he is an antagonist and not a representative ; for his opinions are opposed to theirs, and their will he will not execute. And this must always be the case when political parties act upon elections and a majority or plurality rule assigns to one party the whole representation of the constituency."

Testimony regarding the working of the system of free voting in Illinois, which will be quoted later, make the following extract from a report made to the British Parliament by Lord Cairns, to show the advantages which would be gained by having minorities represented, appear prophetic. In that report he said :

"You will have from the same constituency two members representing the majority and one representing the minority, communicating freely with each other, and without the slightest tinge of jealousy or apprehension that the interests of one would jar or conflict with the · interests of the other in the constituency. * * * Again, with regard to the constituency itself—and this is one of the most important views of the case—observe the advantages which would be gained : First, I believe that you would gain the greatest possible local satisfaction ; *there is nothing so irksome to those who form the minority of one of those large constituencies as finding that from the mere force of numbers they are virtually excluded from the exercise of any political power;* that it is vain for them to attempt to take any part in public affairs ; that the elections must go in one direction, and that they have no political power whatever. On the one hand the result is great dissatisfaction, and on the other *it is disinclination on the part of those who form the minority to take any part in affairs in which it is important they should take a prominent and conspicuous part."*

Mr. Calhoun, who was a profound student of our institutions and who foresaw some of the dangers in store for us, said * :

" The right of suffrage is, indeed, the indispensable and primary principle ; but it would be a great and dangerous mistake to suppose, as many do, that it is of itself sufficient to form constitutional governments. To this erroneous opinion," he adds, "may be traced one of the causes why so few attempts to form constitutional governments have succeeded ; and why, of the few which have, so small a number have had a durable existence. It has led not only to mistakes in the attempt to form such governments, but to their overthrow, when they have, by some good fortune, been correctly formed. So far from

---

* " A Disquisition on Government."

being of itself sufficient—however well guarded it might be, and however enlightened the people—it would, unaided by other provisions, leave the government as absolute as it would be in the hands of irresponsible rulers, and with a tendency, at least as strong, towards oppression and abuse of its powers. * * * * The dominant party for the time," he repeats, "would have the same tendency to oppression and abuse of power which, without the right of suffrage, irresponsible rulers would have. No reason, indeed, can be assigned why the latter would abuse their power, which would not apply with equal force to the former. The dominant majority for the time would in reality, through the right of suffrage, be the rulers—the controlling, governing, and irresponsible power—and those who make and execute the laws would for the time in reality be but their representatives and agents." And he proceeds to show that the abuse of the power which would thus be acquired could only be counteracted by giving to each division, or interest, through its appropriate organ, a concurrent vote.

The American Proportional Representation League, in an address issued in the first number of its *Quarterly Review* says :

"Thoughtful, earnest citizens are confronted with the fact that wherever reform must be obtained through political action, that action is delayed, if not prevented, by a system of representation which fails to accomplish the purpose for which it was intended. The various reformers, as they approach the law making bodies, whether they be city councils, state legislatures or national congresses and parliaments, find that that branch of government which should reflect in miniature the whole country, instead mirrors the opinions of only a privileged few. Though these reformers may number a considerable part of the body politic, they find it impossible to secure representation in the halls of legislature.

"The effect of this state of affairs has been to create a feeling of recklessness on the part of some men and of apathy on the part of others. Some propose to right their grievances by force ; others give up the fight and withdraw from the field in disgust. All are prone to despair when they realize the Herculean task of securing a hearing of the so-called representatives of the people."

CHAPTER VI.

FREE VOTING IN ILLINOIS.

In propounding a system of free voting as a remedy for some of the evils which have been described the objection is often made by those who have little or no knowledge of any such systems that they are all "theoretical," "impracticable," or "academic," and are altogether unworkable, and as a climax to such arguments those who use them call all who advocate any such system "doctrinaires." Practical politicians and chronic objectors, who are ignorant of the fact that this system has been in successful use in Illinois, and elsewhere, for more than twenty years, tell us with great assumption of superior wisdom that such schemes are all very well in theory, but in practice they will not work, and have a great deal to say about ignorant voters, corrupt election inspectors, wily politicians and general popular stupidity. Fractional votes are especially objected to, on the ground that ignorant voters could not comprehend them, and that stupid inspectors of election could not count them; and that such a system of voting would open the door to much corruption, and would facilitate and lead to miscounting. For the reason that such objections are so frequently made and in order to get some testimony with reference to the practical difficulties encountered in the operation of the system, the third question in the circular of inquiry was propounded. This was as follows:

3d. *Is there any practical difficulty in the operation of the system, either through the ignorance of voters, or of inspectors of election, in counting the votes, or in any other way?*

To this a very large majority of those who replied answered it with a simple negative, and gave testimony that there was no practical difficulty in the operation of the system, and only a very small proportion of those who answered spoke of any trouble at all. The following are a few of the answers received:

"Was at first, as with all new rules, but none are now experienced." Rep. *Beardstown.*

"I think not. It is easily learned and used, and the inspectors learn to count such votes readily." Rep. *Naperville.*

"None to speak of. Voters sometimes wish to change their votes and ask for instruction. In my experience for eight years as a town officer do not remember of a lost vote." Rep. *Carrollton.*

"No ; the difficulties feared with regard to counting of votes under the various systems proposed by reformers are about wholly imaginary." Dem. *Chicago.*

"No ; I have served on many boards—no trouble at all." Dem. *Charleston.*

"Not in this state. The tickets being printed thus—if three representatives, two on majority and one on minority. The majority tickets give 1½ votes to each candidate, the minority 3 votes to its candidate." Rep. *Virden.*

"None. 1½ votes each are placed on the ballots opposite the majority candidates' names, and 3 votes opposite the name of the minority candidate." Rep. *Manchester.*

"None whatever. All understand it and everything works like a charm. Tickets are printed 1½ votes for *A* and *B* each and 3 votes for *C* and thus there is no trouble." Rep. *Joliet.*

"It has always been very simple at our place as the majority party get two out of three representives, they print their tickets:

John Jones, 1½ votes.
Frank Link, 1½ votes."

Rep. *Paris.*

"No difficulty in either point or in any respect. The central committee generally has one vote for each of three candidates printed on the ticket, 1½ if two, or three votes if only one candidate." Rep. *Naperville.*

"If strict party ticket is voted by electors, no difficulty. In off years under the Australian ballot system some difficulty is experienced by ' *scratchers* ' and there is the mischief to play often." Rep. *East St. Louis.*

"Under the Australian system the ignorant or timid voter votes the ticket as printed, whereas if they had intelligence or confidence they would plump on one candidate. Counting is no objection." *Joliet.*

" None upon which any opposition to the system could be based. There is certainly some difficulty inasmuch as it taxes the attention of election clerks more severely than a simpler system." Dem. *East St. Louis.*

A few—not exceeding a half dozen—of those who have replied to the inquiries in the circular say that there is some difficulty in working cumulative voting with the Australian ballot system, or was, when the latter was first introduced. A few more of the respondents say that sometimes inspectors of election have difficulty in counting up fractional votes, but the general tenor of the testimony collected from all parts of the state shows in the most indisputable way, that there is no practical difficulty at all in the operation of this method of voting. It may be " theoretical," it may be " academic," and not in accord with the tenets or interests of " practical politics," nevertheless it works with little or no friction, and it only needs the lubrication of the good will of those who believe in justice and righteousness as principles which should control the adminstration of government to make it work satisfactorily anywhere. To those who recklessly stigmatize the system as " impracticable " and " unworkable," and who generally belong to that large class of people who deem it superfluous to consider whether any measure is right or wrong, wise or unwise before condemning it, it may be said that twenty-two years of favorable experience with this system, in a great state like Illinois, is strong testimony to prove that at least it is *practicable,* and to the charge that it is "unworkable" it may be answered that *it does work* and *has worked* successfully and satisfactorily for nearly a quarter of a century, in communities differing as widely in their characteristics as the rural districts of " Egypt " * do from the cosmopolitan society of Chicago.

To get the general opinions of people familiar with the working of cumulative voting in Illinois, of the merits and advantages of that system as exemplified by its operation in that state, the following question was included in the circular of inquiry :

6th. " *Do you consider the system* (of cumulative voting) *a fair and just one to all parties concerned ; does it promote good government, or is*

---

* The southern part of Illinois is jocosely called " Egypt."

the old system, now in use in all other states, of electing only one representative from each district and giving each voter only one vote to be preferred ?".

One hundred and thirty-six replies were received to the circular. Of these 68 came from Republicans, 43 of whom were decidedly in favor of the Illinois system of cumulative voting, 20 were opposed to it and 5 were doubtful. Of the 58 Democrats who answered 43 were in favor of, 9 were opposed to, and 6 were doubtful concerning its merits. Four Prohibitionists were in favor and 1 opposed to it ; the 3 Independents and 2 Populists were all in favor of it. The opinions therefore as expressed by respondents to the circular, who were scattered all over the state, were 95 in favor, 30 opposed to and 11 doubtful about the merits of cumulative or free voting.

Quotations from some of the answers received to the question last quoted will be a tolerably good indication of the opinions of people in Illinois with reference to the advantages and disadvantages of the system of voting and electing representatives in their state. A considerable proportion of those who answered the question simply expressed their preference of the cumulative plan to the old method of electing single representatives. The following replies will, however, give some idea of how it is regarded by persons interested in the administration of public affairs in that state :

"All things considered, it is a good system. It keeps both parties alert in every corner of the state, and the minority gets its deserts rather better than it otherwise could." Independent. *Chicago.*

" It helps in that it prevents a big party majority. For instance, in the Illinois senate Democrats have a good working majority. In the House they have so little that the members must all attend." Mugwump. *Decatur.*

"All are satisfied apparently with the law and its workings." Prohibitionist. *Bunker Hill.*

"It is better than the old plan, but not so effective nor just and wise as the quota system would be. *There are no objections to the Illinois law that could not be remedied by an extension of the idea,* so as to give minority parties representation in law-making bodies, and at the same time do entire justice to majorities." Populist. *Joliet.*

" In my opinion it is the best and fairest system ever devised to obtain a representation of all parties. I was a member of the Constitutional Convention which adopted the minority plan in 1870, and I have also served as a member of the state senate in 1877 and 1879, and have had an opportunity of seeing the practical working of the scheme, and I have found that the best members of the lower house were formed of the minority members, and that the best character of the legislation was favored by them and enacted into laws through their efforts and influence. Through them corrupt legislation and the efforts of the ward politicians of cities, of the majority party who break into the legislature by party strength can be checkmated and prevented." Dem. *Carmi.*

" I think our system a fair one and that it is here to stay. The cumulative system of voting has the distinct advantage of being an obstacle in the way of gerrymandering and other schemes of professional politicians." Dem. *Havana.*

" I think our way the better. It is a good law because it permits the minority party to have a representative to look after their interests and introduces measures beneficial to that party. *It causes the masses to take more interest in legislation* and this is the only hope of our country. Every party should be able to invite investigation." Dem. *Jerseyville.*

" I have had doubts on the subject, but I believe I would not favor a change from the present mode. By cumulative voting both parties in each district are pretty certain to be represented in the legislature, so that the *whole people of each district is more likely to take an interest in the legislature* than if a portion of such people had *no* representative of their political faith. The representatives themselves will be in consultation with the people and work up this interest which I deem beneficial. People like to consult representatives of their own political faith." Dem. *East St. Louis.*

" I prefer the cumulative system as used in this state. Our several tickets are printed on one sheet of paper, Dem., Rep., Peo. and Pro. A voter can cast three votes for any of the candidates, or can vote one vote for three candidates, or one-and-a-half votes for two candidates. In my opinion it is an excellent system or method of voting." Dem. *Augusta.*

"We think the system a fair one and to be preferred to the old system. In districts close politically each party is compelled to select wisely as to men and to urge an equal divide in voting, or suffer for failure to do so. In other districts poor material and the conduct and result of campaign cannot be said to be improved by our Illinois method." Dem. *Murphysboro*.

"I think it is the best system that can be adopted all things considered. In this state it gives the minority a chance to be heard in the legislature and if they but send good men then they can accomplish much. I am decidedly in favor of the system as in vogue here and would not consent to a change back to the old way. We certainly get as good and as intelligent representatives, and in every district in the state the system gives the minority party an opportunity to be repre- sented. My advice is to adopt it in every state." Dem. *Joliet*.

"I consider the system fair and better than the old system. I have had a great deal of actual experience in cumulative voting, hav- ing been elected to our General Assembly five times. It gives both parties a representative from all sections of the state. It insures the elec- tion of better men, as they are compelled to run over a large district, and must of necessity be men of standing at home and acquaintance abroad. It is usually the unpopular candidate on the ticket that runs ahead, as he may induce his friends to cast three votes for him, while the popular candidate will urge an equal division of the votes." Dem. *McLanesboro*.

"It is fair and just as far as it goes, and an improvement on the old system and is better than the old, but it makes party lines too close. We do not get a perfectly representative body. The 'quota' system gives a perfect representative body and in addition does away with the gerrymander." Dem. *Elgin*.

"I think the system fair and *it operates to make a change of control easier to accomplish*." Dem. *Decatur*.

"I prefer our system as it insures the minority a representation large enough to criticise with effect." Dem. *Alton*.

"It is a most fair system to all, and much preferable to the old method. Get a copy of the Illinois law and adopt it as it is together with the Australian system of voting." Dem. *Mattoon*.

" Yes ; I think the minority system is the better, for under it nei-
ther party ever obtains an overwhelming majority in the legislat··re.
Its merit is that each party has nearly the same representation in the
General Assembly, the majority for either being small." Dem. *Austin,
Cook Co.*

" I consider the system a fair one for all parties, as it gives all a
chance to secure representatives in the legislature." Dem. *Chester.*

" It is a good plan in the right direction—not perfect but to be
progressed. The old system is certainly not to be preferred. *All* the
people should be represented in *all* legislative assemblies. The system
as to minority representation and cumulative voting in Illinois has
produced good results and is in the right direction, though not yet
perfect in details of operation." Tariff Reform Dem. *Chicago.*

" I like the minority plan. Its sole merit is that it gives all the
people everywhere a representation, that it more nearly voices the
people than the majority plan." Dem. *Carlyle.*

" Yes ; prefer the Illinois system, think it promotes good government." Dem. *Pontiac.*

" I can conceive of nothing better or fairer in the way of representing the people in the popular branch of a state legislature, and
think it far better than the old one of electing one member from each
district. One advantage, in my opinion, is the tendency to lessen the
expenditure of money in the canvass preceding election. To some
extent this expenditure is made in the primary canvass, but the evils
resulting from it are not nearly so great or perceptible." Dem. *Jacksonville.*

" I feel sure that I am right in saying that the voters of our state
would not consider a proposition to change the law. After a trial since
1870, I feel sure that it is universally satisfactory. There is always a
good minority representation, which is surely a good thing for the
people." Dem. *Monmouth.*

" The system is fair, and is to be commended more on account of
giving all classes representation than for any other cause." Dem.
Metropolis.

" Think it somewhat to be preferred, as giving minorities in cities
and counties a hearing. It does not greatly change political com-

plexion of our legislature, but parties have representatives from all parts of the state, instead of from the strongholds only." Dem. *Quincy.*

" I consider the system far superior to the old and believe that the people are thus better represented." Dem. *Macomb.*

" Yes ; it makes the parties careful to nominate stronger men, than they would if one party had a big majority, and yet very shallow men, as a rule, run for the House." Dem. *Charleston.*

" I think that this system combined with the Australian ballot system gives the people an opportunity to choose the best men nominated regardless of party politics. Any man with an objectionable record, placed in nomination by either party, would be minus votes at the final count of ballots. Dem. *East St. Louis.*

The following are answers received from Republicans.

" It is eminently fair and just to all parties, and tends to promote good government because it gives all views of *respectable* following a chance to be heard, and, from a non-partisan view is to be preferred. It insures a fair representation of the minority in spite of gerrymander. In the districts where the strength of the parties is not equally divided and the strength of neither party will justify placing three candidates on their ticket, the majority party usually nominates two and the minority but one candidate ; the fight having been settled in the primaries. If nearly even, each party puts up two and the unpopular or unfit candidate must go. The same when the strength is such that one party puts up three and the other two candidates, thus forcing the selection of good men. Put up a good man and a bad one on the same ticket, if his party gives the good one three votes it will defeat the bad one." Rep. *Carmi.*

" There is room for more than one opinion here, but as a general thing the plan is satisfactory. I think *the objections to the plan come from the majority party* as the law works to the advantage of the minority, giving them better representation." Rep. *Shelbyville.*

" I consider the system fair and just and has a tendency to promote good government. I know that it is better than the old system." Rep. *Altamont.*

" The system is beneficial locally in eliminating partisan bitterness.

As all three of the candidates are sure of election there is no temptation to make a fight against them." Rep. *White Hall.*

"The system seems to work well in our state, since we have got used to it. Take a large section of country where heretofore one party took all. It is now divided which seems to give better satisfaction. Rep. *Paris.*

"I think the present system in Illinois is far preferable to the old system, as in this portion of the state we never had a Republican representative under the old system, but now always have. So when persons have business before the legislature they have some one of their own party to transact their business." Rep. *Effingham.*

"We like our system very much indeed." Rep. *Elgin.*

"Generally I consider that the cumulative system is productive of the best results. Everything considered, in my opinion, the cumulative system, as used in this state is the best that could be adopted." Rep. *Lockport.*

"After twenty years of experience I heartily endorse minority representation. If in a district of 20,000 voters the majority is 200 the two majority men would represent 10,200, the one minority man would represent 9800 voters. I think it is the best system, as far as I have had opportunity to observe that has ever been in practice, for it makes no difference how large a majority there is the minority is sure of a representative."* Rep. *Brooks, Madison Co.*

"I think the cumulative system is as fair a way as an assembly can be chosen. I much prefer it to the old way of electing members." Rep. *Urbana.*

"I am confident that the system works generally to the satisfaction of our people." Rep. *Moline.*

"I like the system, think it the best. Its tendency is good—it causes thought and care in presenting candidates." Rep. *Beardstown.*

"The system is fair and just. I have never heard a wish among intelligent men to return to the old system." Rep. *Dixon.*

"The system is a good one. I believe in minority representation and this secures it. It is a great improvement over the old system.

---

* A minority must have *more* than a fourth of the votes to be sure of a representative.

Because I have the power in belonging to a majority party is no reason why I should disfranchise my neighbor who belongs to a minority party." Rep. *Joliet.*

" I consider our system a very just one, from the fact that the minority party has from all parts of the state a representation, and small and independent parties have the same chance as in other systems." Rep. *Carrollton.*

" The cumulative system is good because it induces party organization in each district; hence each side is more or less watched. Also it gives representation to all shades of opinion from every part of the state. The more country representatives in the legislature the better." Rep. *Beardstown.*

" I have served in the Illinois senate over forty years ago in the same district with Abraham Lincoln in which he was elected to the House during my term. The system is eminently fair and just, especially to minorities, insuring representation to parties that are in bare minority, and double representation to the majority." Rep. *Havana.*

" Yes ; I think it is preferable to the old system, for the reason that the minority party has a representative from each district." Rep. *Virden.*

" I much prefer our present system. I consider the same fair and just to all parties concerned. In our legislative district (which is largely Republican) we elect a Republican senator and two Republican representatives, while the Democrats elect one representative. If it were not for our present system the Democrats would not be represented in our district at all. The Republican convention nominates two and the Democrats one representative. The reverse of this is true in Democratic districts." Rep. *Naperville.*

" Yes, it is fair and just and it makes a better government, as the majority is more careful in making laws, as the majority necessarily is small and the minority keeps them in check. It has given entire satisfaction in our state, and I regard it as a big improvement over the old plan." Rep. *Bushnell.*

" I prefer the minority system. It is good from this point of view ; the parties are more evenly balanced or divided in the legislature and it renders them more careful in legislation." Rep. *Alton.*

" When the system was adopted the southern half of Illinois was decidedly Democratic and the northern counties were just as pronounced Republican. On that account the cumulative system was particularly beneficial, as it gave both sections a better representation than under the old system." Rep. *Dixon.*

" Objections to the system come only from strong partisans who belong to the majority party and who want everything in the way of office which they can get. Until something better can be devised we had better cling to this and extend it as widely as possible." Rep. *Joliet.*

" It seems to me the tendency of the system of cumulative voting is an educational element—it gives power to the weak, hope to reform, clips the wings of party domination, gives the minority a voice in legislation and has a tendency to put better men before the people." Rep. *Beardstown.*

From the testimony which has been presented it may then be fairly claimed for the system of voting adopted in Illinois :

1. That it gives voters three candidates to choose from, all of whom can be elected, instead of only one as in the old method of electing single representatives from each district. In other words it gives more *freedom* and *independence* in the choice of candidates.

2. It secures representation to minorities, which include more than a fourth of the voters in a district, and who unite on a candidate.

3. There is little or no difficulty in the practical operation of the method of voting, either on the part of the voter in giving all his votes to one candidate or in dividing them equally between two or three candidates, or in counting the votes when thus divided.

4. It is an obstacle in the way of, and lessens the evils and chances of gerrymandering.

5. It leads the people generally to take more interest in public affairs, because all can have a part in legislation and the conduct of the government.

6. It makes a change of representation easier to accomplish and " clips the wings of party domination."

7. It gives a minority in the legislature large enough to criticise with effect and influence and hold in check the action of the majority,

and by dividing the representation more equally, makes all more careful in making laws.

8. It is claimed that the minority representatives are generally abler and better men than those elected by the majority, but the testimony relating thereto is conflicting and to some extent contradictory.

9. By giving a more just representation to the two or more parties in each or most districts it lessens party bitterness.

These results are certainly of very great importance in promoting good government. The advantages gained thereby will be more fully discussed later on. There is however an obverse side to this as there is to all questions, which will be referred to in the next chapter.

CHAPTER VII.

Experience in Illinois has indicated some objections to the system of cumulative voting as adopted and practiced there and while the preponderance of public sentiment is strongly in its favor it is not unanimous. Each voter as has been explained, has three votes and can give all three of them to one candidate or $1\frac{1}{2}$ to one and $1\frac{1}{2}$ to another or 1 to each of three. He must designate on his ticket how his votes are to be distributed. This distribution is generally determined by an estimate of the strength of the parties by the party managers. If it is thought that either party has a decisive majority, that party usually nominates two candidates and the other nominates one. If the parties are nearly equally divided they each nominate two. In the former case, the nomination is generally equivalent to an election. In the last if either party has more votes than its opponents and if those votes are equally divided between its two candidates they will both be elected. Thus suppose the Republicans have 3637 votes and the Democrats 3636 and the former nominate A and B as candidates and the democrats nominate C and D—now if the Republicans all cast $1\frac{1}{2}$ votes for A and $1\frac{1}{2}$ for B they will each have $5455\frac{1}{2}$ votes. If the Democrats do the same thing for C and D they will each have 5454 votes, and both Democrats will be elected and one Republican. If however two of the Republicans should " plump " for A—that is give all three of their votes to him—then A would have $5458\frac{1}{2}$ votes, B $5453\frac{1}{2}$, C 5454, and D 5454. Consequently A and C and D would have the highest vote and B would be defeated. In other words only one of the Democrats and both of the Republicans would be elected. It will thus be seen that where there is any doubt about which party has the largest vote a candidate may secure his election easier by taking votes from and defeating his colleague than to get them from his opponent. It therefore may become and often is a contest between colleagues instead of between political antagonists. That this actually does occur is abundantly shown by the replies received to our fifth enquiry which was as follows :

5th. *It has been objected to this system that if a very popular man is nominated that an undue proportion of the votes in his district may be concentrated on him and that the remaining two candidates might thus be elected by a minority—in your experience is this often or ever the case ?*

A Republican correspondent graphically describes what sometimes occurs under the circumstances. He says :

" When a district is very nearly equal in political strength but two men are usually nominated on each side. A very popular candidate is liable to gather votes from his running mate, and thus put them so far apart that their two adversaries will run in between them, especially if they are well matched and run well together or in a bunch, and it happens in every campaign in this state, that a majority candidate is slaughtered, and although it seldom affects the result politically, for the reason that such accidents come to both sides, yet it leads to bad blood and open accusations of bad faith.

" The system puts a nominating convention on its good behavior when it comes to nominating candidates. They must see to it that their candidates are well yoked and well matched for running ; for to win they must keep neck and neck. If the city population preponderates in the district it is poor policy to put a city and country candidate in the same team. A stampede would put the farmer far in the lead. In a manufacturing district a labor man with a farmer or a lawyer or merchant makes a poor team to manage. A churchman and a sport won't work. A kid and an old man is no better. A native and a naturalized person is sure defeat for one or the other in a close district. In making nominations the convention must find pairs with respect to all the usual and ordinary elements entering into a hot political campaign. A candidate that runs too far ahead is just as dangerours to *his* party as the man who runs far behind, which is not the case in the old system. Under the latter the man runs ahead does so at the expense of his adversary, but under the cumulative system it is at the expense of his colleague. His best friends and admirers, politically, plump three votes, *which takes ½ from his colleague* and that, too, when it is not necessary to elect him, The fear that *he* might get left induces his friends to plump, *just to keep him abreast* with his colleague.

"A great deal of plumping is done in every election, but if it is caused by natural causes, such as location, trade, profession, nationality, color or social standing, the candidates come out even if they both are on an equality and evenly matched. If both are from the country or from the city, each will receive about the same number of plumpers in his locality. If both are mechanics the labor unions will divide fairly between them. If both are German, Irish, or natives, their several clans will deal fair with them.

"Whatever advantage or disadvantage there is in the system, it will accrue to both parties alike ; and I can't see why if one party should be for it the other should be against it.

"The weak point in the system is that it breeds suspicion, jealousy, and bad blood between the candidates, and sometimes leads to an open rupture among political friends. With two candidates on a side and only three seats to fill, one candidate will be left. Undue zeal or popularity on the part of one may defeat his colleague. A stampede which both sides are working for may produce the same result." Rep. *Ottawa.*

Other correspondents confirm this testimony, as will be seen from the following answers received to the 5th question :

"Probably the greatest objection to be urged against the system is 'plumping,' which sometimes defeats one of the majority candidates, as it is found both could have been elected if the voting had been fair." Dem. *Henry.*

"The difficulty in the cumulative voting is that the friends of candidates will 'plump,' and thus it has happened that the majority party would only elect one out of three, by the friends of the successful candidates plumping, who would thus receive many more votes than enough to elect." Rep. *Moline.*

"One of my objections is that it hinders a fair stand-up fight between parties and candidates. It is as frequently as not a fight between two candidates on the same ticket rather than between candidates on opposing tickets. It is easier for a candidate to gain his election at the expense of his colleague than at the expense of the opposing party." Dem. *Freeport.*

"It has frequently happened that the majority party, with plenty of votes to elect its two candidates, has elected but one, because his friends ran him far ahead to make it appear that he was very popular, or for other personal reasons, and the party entitled to but one representative secured two. * * * In the close districts, where each party names two candidates, its working is always uncertain and leads to attempts at all kinds of trickery.   In the safe districts the majority party never names more than two candidates, and thus insures their election, and the minority usually names but one, so that the voters really have no choice, as these then are sure to be elected.'' Rep. *Springfield.*

'' The plan in Illinois has been the means of provoking a great deal of ' bad blood ' between the friends of a successful candidate and those of one who was defeated on the same ticket, resulting in frequently giving the minority two representatives.   Again with two candidates in the field, one a good and capable man, the other incapable and perhaps disreputable, the disposition of party leaders is to make a hard fight for the latter, who is deemed the weaker, in order to save party supremacy, and not infrequently with the result that the good man is defeated and the unworthy candidate elected.'' Rep. *Warsaw.*

'' I think it has become the universal custom in Illinois for each party to nominate but two candidates and in this and other counties, where one party is in a hopeless minority, it is a growing custom to nominate but one, as the fight between two men on the same ticket, when only one of them can be elected, leads to divisions and feuds which weaken the whole ticket.'' Rep. *Springfield.*

'' A popular man overbalances his running mate and thus gives to the minority party two out of three representatives ; sometimes the best electioneerer causes the same result.'' Rep. *Warsaw.*

'' The popular man is most likely to ' get there ' by a large majority ; the less popular may be left entirely or merely slip in. The central committee tries to regulate that but does not always succeed.'' Rep. *Naperville.*

'' This sometimes is the case and to my notion is the worst feature in the system.'' Rep. *Alton.*

'' Yes, this occurs rather frequently and is the real objection to the system.   Selfish men use it to their advantage and a popular candidate will, by no fault of his own, defeat his colleague on the same ticket." Rep. *Springfield*.

"The massing of the vote on one candidate may and does, often defeat a worthy colleague." Rep. *West McHenry*.

"In some instances the friends of a candidate will become scared and 'plump' three votes for him, defeating his running mate." Rep. *Moline*.

"When the district is considered to be close, then the temptation of the candidate's particular friends to 'plump' for him is strong. By this means the minority sometimes secures two members." Rep. *Chicago*.

"Often a good man on the majority side is sacrificed by 'plumping' for the other candidate on the ticket with him." Rep. *Champaign*.

"More opportunity I think as the plumping of three votes for one candidate may elect the worst one of four candidates." Rep. *Austin*.

"When the vote between the parties is very close, each party having two candidates and three to be elected, it results that some popular candidate draws from his running mate and the minority party elects two of the three." Dem. *Carlyle*.

"It is usually the unpopular candidate on the ticket that runs ahead, as he may induce his friends to cast their votes for him, while the popular candidate will urge an equal division of the votes." Dem. *Mc Leansboro*.

"It has quite frequently occurred that the best man of one or the other party was defeated by his competitor on the same ticket who urged his friends to give him three votes as he otherwise would be beaten." Dem. *Freeport*.

"'Plumping' three votes for one man is common. I have known two members of the minority party to be elected in a district because a candidate of the majority party pulled to himself more than his share of the party vote." Ind. *Chicago*.

"In 1890 in two districts of this state, the 12th and 16th, which were very close the Democratic party lost one candidate in each district because both the leading parties had nominated two candidates each and one of the candidates got his friends to 'plump' for him and he ran away ahead, while the other man with him was defeated when the two combined had many more votes than the two Republican candidates." Dem. *Havana.*

"It is not unusual for the minority to get two of the representatives because of the more popular man on the majority ticket running ahead of his mate. This is liable to happen in close districts." Rep. *Pontiac.*

"This has happened once in this, the 47th district." Dem. *Belleville.*

"This is often the case, and then when the man comes up for re-election every one says, well, so and so is all right, see how many votes he got at the last election—we will just help the weak man, and I have known the really strong man to be defeated in the endeavor to elect both men—it has happened in this district several times." Rep. *East St. Louis.*

"I have seen this same trouble in our district several times." Rep. *Waukegan.*

"There is danger of this unless great precautions are taken by party managers. This has occurred here." Rep. *Elgin.*

"This happened in Iroquois or Kankakee county in 1890." Dem. *Peoria.*

"When a third party has a candidate it sometimes happens that one of the two majority candidates plays the other false and through his 'workers' has three votes cast straight for himself and the third party man may slip in instead of his majority party colleague." Dem. *Shelbyville.*

"Not often, but is sometimes; not always because the man is popular, but that he is active, and works. This is a very serious objection to my mind." Rep. *Moline.*

"This is an objection undoubtedly." Dem. *Carthage.*

"Does not give third and fourth minority candidates a chance. It is very unsatisfactory in its results because very often good men are defeated by too many votes being cast for one man of the two usually nominated by the two old parties. * * * *The only practical difficulty is that a voter cannot tell when he is casting more votes than a favorite candidate needs.*" Pop. *Joliet.*

That the direct evils resulting from "plumping" however are not very serious is indicated by the fact that in 1892 there was but one district (Fig. 4, p. 23) in which a minority party elected two representatives and the majority only one. This occurred in the sixth district, when the Democrats cast 61,637 votes and elected only one representative, and the Republicans with only 51,685 votes elected two. It will be noticed that correspondents mention some other cases which occurred at other elections, but such instances appear to be comparatively infrequent, and about two-thirds of those who answered the inquiry say that it seldom or never occurs that the minority party in a district elects a majority of the representatives. One Populist in Joliet says : " It has happened three or four times in fifteen years." The worst evil resulting therefrom is probably the sense of injury or injustice produced in the minds of persons with a strong feeling of party fealty or allegiance. As one of the correspondents says : " It breeds suspicion, jealousy and bad blood between the candidates, and sometimes leads to open rupture among political friends." Others say : " It leads to all kinds of trickery " ; and " to divisions and feuds which weaken the whole ticket." The instance mentioned by the correspondent from Warsaw indicates how a good man may be sacrificed by party leaders for another candidate who is incapable and perhaps unworthy. The whole matter is summed up by the correspondent from Joliet who says that *" the only practical difficulty is that a voter cannot tell when he is casting more votes than a favorite candidate needs."* and another points out that the Illinois system " gives the minority party representation when the *guess* of the minority and the *guess* of the majority in nominating conventions are correct."

Any element in a system of electing representatives which makes the results depend—even to a limited extent—on correct guessing or chance will not commend itself to those who want good government. It will be shown later on that the uncertainty in the working of cumulative voting due to such causes would be very much greater if the number of representatives to be elected from each district was increased, so that more than three were elected in each district. The reason for increasing the number by enlarging the districts will be pointed out later, but without doing so now it will be apparent that if,

say seven representatives are elected from each district, voters would be
more perplexed to know whether to give all their votes to one candidate or divide them between two, three, four or more, than they would
be if only three are elected, when usually the only question to be decided is whether to give all their votes to one man or divide them
between two candidates.   If this difficulty of cumulative voting could
be overcome the perplexity of the voter and the objection which has
been made to the system, that there is an element of uncertainty and
some chance involved in the result, would both be obviated, and by
removing the fortuitous feature the voter could exercise his privilege
with more knowledge and freedom.

It sometimes happens though that the character of a man or a
measure are indicated by the enemies he or it makes.   The *opposition*
to cumulative voting may possibly be indicative of its merits as well as
of its demerits.   The testimony elicited by the circular of inquiry may
perhaps throw some side light on the subject.   Thus a Republican
says :

"I think the objections to the plan come from the majority party
as the law works to the advantage of the minority, giving them better
representation."   Rep. *Shelbyville.*

Another Republican from *Rock Island* says :

" From the standpoint of minority representation it is very satisfactory ; from a partisan standpoint it is an advantage to the Democratic party, as it gives them a larger representation in the House than
they would otherwise have.   The northern two-thirds of Illinois is
mainly Republican and the southern end ('Egypt') Democratic, and
the larger population is north."

" I think the system a fairly good one.   Objections to it come only
from strong partisans who belong to the majority party and who want
everything in the way of office which they can get."   Rep. *Joliet.*

As Illinois is ordinarily a Republican state it can perhaps be understood why some persons of that faith are inclined to oppose a system
which lessens their political influence and power.   To those who are
inclined towards the side of justice and righteousness, in the administration of political affairs, the objections of these opponents of
cumulative voting become arguments in its favor.

But it has also been objected to the Illinois system that under it it is difficult if not impossible for third or independent parties to elect candidates. The following is some of the testimony of correspondents with reference to that point:

" Our system is called minority representation but never but once has a third party candidate been elected from this, Will county, in twenty years." Populist. *Joliet.*

" From the standpoint of the two parties it does, but when a third party is a factor, unless aggregating a given number of votes it does not, I think." People's Party. *Abingdon, Knox Co.*

" I believe that the quota system in some form would improve matters and at least give the minorities, now virtually disfranchised, a voice in government." Prohibition. *Geneva.*

In the election in Illinois in 1892 not a single third party member was sent to the House of Representatives, although the Prohibitionists had 24,684 votes and the People's Party 20,108 out of a total of 872,948. The quota which should have elected a member of the legislature was 5705, so that if those parties could have concentrated their votes the one could have elected four and the other three members. There is no report that any candidate was elected in opposition to the two dominant parties. It will thus be seen that in Illinois there is only a *limited amount of freedom* in voting. The remedy for this and some of the other evils which have been pointed out is to increase the size of the districts and the number of representatives to be elected from each, as will be more fully shown farther on.

Another objection to the system of cumulative voting, in use in Illinois, has been pointed out by persons familiar with its operation in that state. The following quotations bearing on this objection are given from the answers received to the circular of inquiry. A Democrat in Chicago says:

" The party in majority usually puts up two candidates, the minority one, very rare that either puts up three. Under these conditions the nomination settles the election—the people practically have nothing to do with the matter. Instead of giving the voters more control of the legislature the opposite result is achieved in so far as anything is accomplished—which is not considerable." Dem. *Chicago.*

" The certainty of election which follows the nomination as made under this system, leads, sometimes I fear, to the election of 'machine politicians' by small political rings." Dem. *Chicago.*

"A nomination is often looked upon as being equivalent to an election, and the result is inferior men are frequently elected. If the district is very close and two men are nominated by each of the two leading parties good men are usually named by both." Dem. *Evanston.*

" There is no contest here only for the nomination. After that the successful candidate has nothing to do but *pay his share of the campaign expenses."* Dem. *Hillsboro.*

" A nomination under this system is equivalent to an election, and nominations are fought for by men who would not dare run under the old system." Dem. *Jacksonville.*

" The only objection is that in districts where there is a large majority either way that nominations on both sides are equivalent to election, because the dominant party will nominate two and the minority one, and of course all are elected." Rep. *Havana.*

" The effect on the nominations and the elections is BAD, the two candidates of the majority party and one from the minority are generally elected no matter who they are nor how they got the nomination." Dem. *Freeport.*

" The nomination of the minority candidate being equivalent to an election, thus the people in convention seeking to put its best men forward." Rep. *Virden.*

" It does not secure better men, but perhaps the reverse, for the nominations being equivalent to election are more likely to be controlled by rings and politicians and there is no incentive to put forward the best men. This is especially true of the minority." Rep. *Pontiac.*

" In nine cases out of ten nomination is equivalent to an election and it is only necessary for candidates to pack the caucuses when they can bid defiance to the voters." Prohibition. *Geneva.*

"Since a nomination is under ordinary circumstances equivalent to an election it becomes a chase of the politicians for nomination." Rep. *Moline.*

" A political ' boss ' secures a minority nomination and prevents a second nomination by his party, thereby insuring his own election without contest. Unless party pressure is strong nominations are made of three candidates for three offices, the whole being cut and dried." Ind. *Chicago.*

" Nominations nearly always mean election and the result is evil." Rep. *Jacksonville.*

" In a district where nomination means election it might be easier to ' get there ' by corrupting the convention than by corrupting the people. Yet it has not been our lot to be troubled by corruption in the convention or elsewhere so far as I know." Rep. *Naperville.*

" In this district nomination is equivalent to election. Two Republicans and one Democrat being sure of election—*other* minority parties have no chance." Dem. *Elgin.*

" There is no more opportunity for bribery and corruption and less occasion, since there are usually only three candidates nominated—all of whom are sure of election." Prohib. *Geneva.*

The evil indicated in the testimony which has been quoted it must be admitted, is a serious one, but is one which might have been and was anticipated by those who had studied the subject carefully. The reason for this will be apparent if it is observed that more than a fourth of the voters under this system can always elect a candidate, if they concentrate their votes on him, no matter how their opponents may use their votes and the latter if they have a bare majority, by dividing their votes equally between two candidates can always elect them both. Consequently under ordinary circumstances, the party in the majority would nominate two candidates, and the minority would nominate one. If either should nominate more they would endanger the success of their ticket. Therefore, if by means of party organization, or other means the proportion of the voters named can be influenced, so as to give their votes for the respective party tickets, then the two nominees on the one ticket and the one on the other would be sure of election. If the parties are nearly equally divided then each would probably nominate two candidates. One of them would of course be defeated. With three candidates all of them will be quite certain to be elected. With four only one will be defeated.

Is the evil which has been pointed out by our respondents in Illinois and was foreseen by Mr. Sterne, and others, inherent in the system of minority representation or is it only a defect in the method adopted in that State which is remediable ? The tyranny from which we are all suffering, majorities, minorities and individuals alike, is that of parties, party managers, caucuses, " machines " and " bosses." Apparently the voters in Illinois have in some respects but little more freedom from party domination than voters have where cumulative voting does not prevail.

To ascertain what influence, if any, the Illinois system of cumulative voting exerted in the selection of men for office the following question was propounded in the circular of inquiry :

2d. *What effect does it* (the Illinois system) *have on the nomination of candidates for office ? In other words, are better and more intelligent candidates nominated and elected than were chosen under the old system of electing one member from each district ?*

About two-thirds of those who replied said that they could not see that it had any influence on the selection of candidates, or that better men were selected now than under the old method of electing single members from each district. About a quarter of the respondents said there was a decided improvement in the character of the candidates nominated, and about a tenth of the replies expressed the opinion that the men chosen for representatives under the present Illinois system were worse than those who were formerly selected.

The following are some of the optimistic answers :

" The minority candidates are usually more capable men than were selected under the old plan." Rep. *White Hall.*

" In my opinion it has so operated. The nomination of the minority candidate being equivalent to an election, thus the people in convention seeking to put its best men forward." Rep. *Virden.*

" This system perhaps has the effect of giving us better men than the other, but the best men do not go to the legislature under either system." Rep. *Springfield.*

" In close districts it has a tendency to make the party which ordinarily has the small majority nominate two strong candidates for fear one may be beaten. While stronger candidates are not always better and more intelligent in the long run they probably would be." Rep. *Springfield*.

" In the rural districts I am satisfied we get better candidates as a rule—that is, the minority does." Rep. *Shelbyville*.

" In this particular, no effect, except where the majority is small." Rep. *Quincy*.

" The minority party generally puts up a good man.   Having lived in a locality a long time where the majority party takes everything, if the minority get a chance they generally select the best material, as it is their first opportunity to get a man in." Rep. *Paris*.

" It compels good nominations in all districts where the minority party has more than forty per cent. of the vote.   A poor nomination by either side would lose a seat to the majority, and it would destroy all chance of winning a seat to the minority." Rep. *Ottawa*.

" The action of the law compels parties to be very careful in their nominations and usually the best of men are selected for candidates." Dem. *Mattoon*.

" Usually so.   The most available candidate is sometimes selected but usually the best and most intelligent are put forward." Dem. *Joliet*.

" If it has any effect at all on nominations its tendency is to bring out the best from each party, as a nomination, except in very close districts, where four are made, is about equivalent to an election, and this fact tends to make the contest for nomination more active, thus interesting a larger number of people in the respective parties." Dem. *Jacksonville*.

" The minority party generally sends a good man—the majority, if small, usually selects two popular men fearing the other party will nominate two and elect.   In such cases there is some improvement over the other system." Rep. *Havana*.

" I think we select better men.   The reason is that we have a larger territory to select from." Rep. *Effingham*.

" I believe that the minority party of a district is more apt to nominate a better man than under the old system.   It certainly has no bad tendencies in that regard." Rep. *Dixon*.

" Without doubt better men are nominated.   The parties cannot

afford to put up a bad man as the independent vote would reach him.''
Rep. *Collinsville*.

'' I have not perceived that it causes any better or more intelligent
men to be nominated than under the old system.   The minority member, however, is frequently an able man, and superior to the majority
members of his district in ability and intelligence.''   Rep. *Chicago*.

'' Yes ; especially is this true of the minority candidates, and generally as to both or all party candidates having a chance of election,
the reason partly that good men will not accept nomination for
office when there is no chance of election.   It frequently happens
that only enough candidates are placed in nomination to fill the three
places.''   Rep. *Carmi*.

'' It induces the strong party to be careful to bring out good men,
at least popular ones, or the minority may secure the election of the
majority of candidates by running the most popular candidates.''   Rep.
Beardstown.

The following are some of the opinions of pessimistic respondents
to the question asked.

'' It is very unsatisfactory in its results because very often good
men are defeated by too many votes being cast for one man of the two
usually nominated by the two old parties.   I would not advise New
York or any other state to follow the Illinois law.   *Proportional Representation* is the only true basis to work on.   The Gove or any feasi-
ble application of the principle of quota or proportional voting.''
Pop. *Joliet*.

'' Sometimes yes, sometimes no.   It frequently has this effect : A
political 'boss' secures a minority nomination and prevents a second
nomination by his party, thereby insuring his own election without
contest.   Unless party pressure is strong nominations are made of three
candidates for three offices, the whole being cut and dried.''   Ind.
Chicago.

'' Makes this matter much worse.   Leads directly to deals between
politicians of both (opposing) parties.   This occurs particularly in
cities.   The minority party puts up only one candidate of course, and
the 'gang' runs the primaries.   The 'gang' does not belong to one
party, but is made up of the 'active' men of both.''   Dem. *Chicago*.

"A nomination under this system is equivalent to an election, and nominations are fought for by men who would not dare run under the old system. My opinion is that the candidates under this system are not so good as under the old." Dem. *Jacksonville.*

"Not having lived in Illinois under the old system I can only compare it with other states and see no advantage. Think the tendency is the other way, since in nine cases out of ten nomination is equivalent to an election, and it is only necessary for candidates to pack the caucuses when they can bid defiance to the voters." Prohib. *Geneva.*

"I believe the effect on the nominations and the elections is BAD ; the two candidates of the majority party and one from the minority are generally elected, no matter who they are, nor how they got the nomination." Dem. *Freeport.*

It will be apparent though and was pointed out by Mr. Sterne and others that if the districts were made large enough, so that small minorities could have representation, there would be a corresponding increase of *freedom* to the voter. Obviously the voter will be freer to choose, if he can select from five or seven candidates to be elected in a large district, than he would be if his choice is limited to one or three to be elected from a small one. If for example five members are elected from a district, then one-sixth of the voters + 1 can always elect a candidate by the cumulative plan, whereas if only three are elected, it will require one-fourth of the votes + 1 to succeed. If there are seven then one-eighth + 1 can elect. In other words it is plain that a smaller fraction of *all* the voters in a district are required to elect if there are many candidates, than if there are only a few. It has been pointed out before that it will be easier to influence a sixth of the voters in a large district than a quarter or a half in smaller ones. With five members to elect the majority party might have three and the minority two—if seven were elected they could be divided into groups of four, and three, or some other proportion. This would give very much greater freedom of choice, not only *within the parties* but also to independent voters, and it is also certain that if it were possible for a fourth, a sixth, or an eighth of the voters in a district to nominate and elect a candidate party managers would be cautious about presenting men who are obviously unfit and this would lead to the selection of better candidates.

In other words the larger the districts, and the greater the number of members elected from each of them, the *freer* will be the choice of the electors, and the larger the number of members elected by each party in each district, the greater the freedom and independence of choice within the parties. Different sections, shades of opinion, interests, views and principles, in the same party, may then each have their representatives, under such a system, and at the same time with a greater freedom of choice it might not be necessary for any to surrender allegiance to their common party flag, but they could elect a member of their own party who would satisfactorily represent the special views and interests of those who are not satisfied with other nominees.

It should, perhaps, be made perfectly plain here again that an increase of the number of members to be elected from each district does not necessarily imply an increase in the total number to be elected, but only an increase in the *size* or a consolidation of existing districts. Thus in the State of New York, there are at present 128 assembly districts. If it should be determined to elect five members from each district, the present ones could be consolidated into say twenty-six, making the total number of assemblymen 130; or if it should be decided to elect seven from each, they could be consolidated so as to form say twenty districts, which would give 140 members.

To ascertain the views of persons in Illinois familiar with the working of cumulative voting in that state with reference to the advisability and practicability of enlarging the districts' in that state the 7th question was asked in the circular of inquiry :

7th. *Would it be advantageous to increase the size of the districts so as to elect five, seven or more representatives from each, and give the voter the privilege of casting as many votes as there are representatives to be elected, and cumulate them as he chooses ?*

A very large majority of those who replied to the circular were opposed to any increase in the size of districts and the number of representatives to be elected from each and say they can see no advantage in such a change. A few who have been students of the principles of proportional representation were, however, decidedly in favor of such an increase. Evidently the majority of the correspondents regarded such a change as an innovation for which they saw no good reason. The arguments urged against it were that it would make the system of voting more cumbrous, complicated and confusing. One or two thought that it would facilitate bribery, add to the cost of the campaign, and one correspondent wrote : "The districts are large enough. A voter, too far away from his candidate, is apt to stay in his corn-field, and not go out at election." An increase in the number of members to be elected would undoubtedly add to the difficulties of conducting elections by cumulative voting, but these difficulties it is thought would be entirely obviated if the Burnitz system of counting votes, which will be explained, was adopted, as will be shown farther on.

There are however some other difficulties which will be encountered, with any system, if the districts are enlarged, and there are some limitations and restrictions which appear desirable and should be placed on the number of representatives to be elected from each.

In the first place, if too many candidates are presented, electors will not take an interest in *all* whom they must select from. The average voter may be concerned in the qualifications, characters, opinions and political principles of two or three candidates to be voted for, and may extend that interest to five or seven, but when required to look into the antecedents of a dozen or twenty men, the duty will likely be performed in a very perfunctory manner. Ordinary men are soon wearied by public duties, and will give but little time or thought or labor to them.

There can be no doubt too, as has already been pointed out, that the larger the number of candidates elected from each district by the cumulative system, the greater will be the difficulties of assigning, distributing and counting votes. Under that system, as has been shown, parties must estimate their strength before the elections, and must be guided by such estimates in determining how many candidates to nominate and how to distribute the votes which they can control. With three members to be elected, it is usually only a question whether to nominate one or two candidates, and the distribution of the votes is correspondingly simple, but if there are five candidates it would be a question for each party whether to put one, two, three or four in the field, and if there were seven to be elected the difficulty would be still greater, and voters would be perplexed and uncertain in determining how many candidates to vote for and how many votes to cast for each. Even in Illinois, as has been shown, with only three members to elect from each district, owing to improper distribution of votes it happens at times that votes are wasted and the minority party elects two candidates and the majority only one. An example of this, which has been referred to, occurred in the sixth district in 1892. At that election the Democrats cast 61,637 votes for their candidate and the Republicans gave 25,957 for one and 25,728 for the second one and thus elected both, although the Democrats had very nearly 10,000 more votes than their successful antagonists. Although this does not occur often in Illinois, yet it can be seen that if greater freedom were given to voters by enlarging the districts and increasing the number of representatives to be elected from each, the liability to such misadventures would be much increased, and it would be correspondingly difficult for parties and individuals to know how to distribute their votes. Thus with seven members to elect and only two parties in the field, even if there was no very great disparity in their respective numbers it would—especially where there was much political agitation—be difficult to know whether either party could elect three, four or five members, and in case of a political revolt, it would often be impossible for the independents or the "regulars" to know whether to run one, two, three or more candidates. A miscalculation might mean total defeat, and the impossibility of knowing how votes should be distributed would often result in their waste.

Most of these difficulties, which are inherent in the system of cumulative voting, as already stated, have been anticipated and commented on by writers and students of this subject. Thus Mr. Sterne in his admirable book, to which the public generally owe so much, says :

"If we make the districts large enough * * * and thus give, by the cumulative plan, a representative to any small minority in the community, there can be no opposition to the plan proposed, except its cumbersomeness ; but with small districts electing but three members it has the disadvantage that, while it gives to the minority one representative, it does not get rid of, but on the contrary makes permanent, party action and party machinery, and, in making a nomination equivalent to an election, removes the corruption from the election to the nominating conventions. The residents of New York have seen such a plan work very badly in the election of their boards of supervisors."

Prof. Ware in an article in *The American Law Review* for January, 1872, said of this branch of the subject:

"The task which it [the cumulative method of voting] imposes upon the elector of dividing his suffrages among his candidates, is one which it is difficult to perform intelligently. In point of fact, it must in most cases be done at haphazard, or upon some arbitrary or fanciful principle, thus giving an arbitrary element a material influence on the result. 'In the different practical trials which this reform has met,' says M. Naville, 'two things have been recognized,—*the excellence of the new principle, and the defective nature of the processes by which it is applied,—processes which impair the liberty of the voter and the justice of the results.*'

"* * * The system is liable to produce most unexpected and undesired results through a waste of votes, and this can only be remedied by a rigid discipline which destroys the freedom of the elector, and practically places the election in the hands of party managers."

Mr. S. Dana Horton * states the objection "that the more popular the candidate the less chance is there of proportional representation. The people's favorite will get plumpers in profusion, many votes will be wasted, and so large a plurality may elect no more officers than a minority. * * * In districts electing three representatives, the special dangers of this, but at the same time also the advantages of any system are reduced to a minimum. *The larger the district the more dangerous the peculiarities of this system.* Were it tried on such a scale as that of congressional elections in Ohio, anything like fairness or proportionality would at first be impossible."

Cumulative voting was adopted for the election of members of

---

* Article on Proportional Representation. *Penn Monthly*, for June, 1873.

English school boards in 1870. The rule as it stands in the Elementary Education Act of that date is as follows :

" At every such election every voter shall be entitled to a number of votes equal to the number of members of the school board to be elected, and may give all such votes to one candidate, or may distribute them among the candidates as he thinks fit."

Some interesting testimony with reference to the practical working of this method of electing members of English school boards has been given.

Commenting on it, Mr. G. Shaw Lefevre, an opponent of minority representation, in an article on that subject in the *Contemporary Review* for May, 1884, says :

" The effect of the system adopted has been to give undue weight to small sections. Majorities and the more powerful sections of the electors have not been able to secure a representation in proportion to their numbers. The difficulties of organizing their voters so as to produce their maximum effect when the members to be elected are many, ranging from five to fifteen, are insuperable, and have ·deterred them from putting forward candidates in proportion to their real strength.

" There has, therefore, been in recent contested elections a wasteful accumulation of votes upon the successful candidate of the more powerful sections, and small groups and sections have consequently been able to secure the return of members, when their numbers did not really entitle them to it. Men have been returned upon boards in this way who have proved to be a power only for mischief. This evil has become more apparent as experience has been gained, and as candidates have found that by obtaining the cumulative votes of a group or section they could be returned without difficulty."

In an article by John Westlake, Q. C., in the *Contemporary Review* for March, 1884, on Proportional Representation, in which the author advocates that principle, he says that its " application to school board elections is well established, but needs reform in detail " and expresses the hope that " the spectacle of its working must influence the controversy as to the parliamentary application."

Continuing, he says :

" Let us turn now to what the rudimentary cumulative vote has failed to do. Each shade of opinion held by a numerous body of electors, though represented, has not had its proportional representation. It is evident that a party which runs more candidates than in proportion to its numbers risks returning fewer candidates than in proportion to its numbers, and not only has this risk been often realized, but often also the fear of it has prevented a party from running its due number of candidates. Again, even when the due number, and that only, has been run, all have not been returned, because the votes of their supporters have not been evenly divided among them. *It would seem as if those who established the cumulative vote had greater faith in the power of organizing than the event has justified.* I will give a few instances of the waste of votes, drawn from the last two general elections for the London School Board, because nine years' practice had preceded even the first of the two, and it may therefore be supposed that the power of organizing had reached as full a development as can be expected. In order to appreciate them thoroughly, it is necessary to explain what is meant by a quota. If 10,000 votes are given at an election, and three members are to be elected, the proportional principle requires that any candidate who has received 2501 votes should be elected, because the remaining 7499 votes cannot be so distributed as to give as many as 2501 to more than two others. A little reflection on this example will show the truth of the following rule : *Divide the number of votes given by the number of members to be elected, plus one ; the quotient, plus one, is the quota, that is, the number of votes which on the proportional principle will entitle a candidate to be elected.* If the quotient is fractional, the quota is the next higher integer.

" Now, in the city of London, in 1879, there were four members to elect and 23,591 good votes were given. Therefore the quota was 4719 ; but the highest on the poll got 7153 votes and one member was elected with 2089, or considerably less than half the quota.

" In the Hackney division, in 1879, there were five members to elect and 60,992 good votes were given. Therefore the quota was 10,166 ; but the highest on the poll had 13,727 votes and one member was elected with 4728, or again less than half the quota.

" In the Lambeth division, in 1882, there were eight members to elect, and 153,142 good votes were given. Therefore the quota was 17,016, but the highest on the poll had 34,896 votes, or more than twice the quota, while two members were elected with 8888 and 8190, or about half the quota.

" It is important to observe that the wasteful accumulation of votes on some candidates leads to the election of others with a very small number of votes, because this is the second point in which the working of the actual school board system is open to objection.   It is desirable that each shade of opinion held by a numerous body of electors should be represented, but it is not desirable that very small bodies should have the power of returning candidates.   If a very small group is composed of the partisans of a real shade of opinion, their exclusion will not shake public confidence in the representative assembly, as that of a large group would do, and they can still propagate their views in the press and at meetings.   More often, however, a very small group is composed of the partisans of a candidate ; and he, again, is often one whose personal qualifications have not recommended him for selection to the great body of those with whom his opinions, so far as he has any, would connect him.   Now few who know anything of the working of assemblies will doubt the importance of keeping bad members out, if possible.   Their power for mischief is increased by their election ten-fold more than the power of an average candidate for good is increased by his election, while an exceptionally good candidate can generally impress himself on a large body of supporters.   It is therefore an additional evil, incidental to the wasteful accumulation of votes on some candidates that it facilitates the success of small combinations in favor of others.   *   *   *   Many, worthy candidates, who represented considerable bodies of opinion, have been left with small fractions of quotas through the undue accumulation of votes on other representatives of the same opinions ; and in the instances I have quoted I have had no reference at all to the worthiness or otherwise of the persons concerned.   I have selected them only to show, by striking examples, that election by too few votes is the necessary accompaniment of election by too many ; and then I leave it to every one's knowledge of human nature to assure him that, among the elections made by too few votes, many must be such as he would regret.

" The direction then, in which the actual school board system of election has to be improved is that of giving some assistance to the power of organizing, which has been found insufficient, while adding as little as possible that is novel to a system which has the great advantage that all are now familiar with it.''

Notwithstanding the objections to cumulative voting which have been pointed out, it is nevertheless believed, that, even in the somewhat imperfect form of the Illinois plan, it has very great advantages —the particulars of which have been set forth in the preceding pages—over our present system of single member districts.   Even with the difficulties which have been pointed out it is thought that if the number of members to be elected in each district, by cumulative votes, were increased to say five or seven, the additional freedom which would thereby be acquired by the voter, would greatly outweigh the disadvantages resulting from the uncertainties and perplexity which he would encounter in the distribution of his votes.   In other words the election of *three* members from each district by cumulative voting is better than our present system of electing only *one* by a majority of the votes ; the election of *five* would be still better and *seven* or a greater number would probably be still more advantageous.   The disadvantages in this system, it is believed, though, may be entirely overcome by a very simple method of voting and counting cumulative votes, the principles of which will be explained in the next chapter.

CHAPTER VIII

Many different plans and methods of voting have been devised and proposed for giving representation to minorities and to voters the greatest amount of freedom, independence and certainty in the results of the exercise of the franchise.

No attempt will be made now to describe or explain all of them. Some of them are very complicated and when they were brought up for consideration in the British Parliament they provoked the remark from John Bright—with which perhaps some persons interested in the subject may sympathize—" that they have this disadvantage, that scarcely any one can understand them."

For the present, what will be said will be confined to an inquiry into the principles which ought to control cumulative voting if it is to be entirely *free*, and to the means of complying with such principles.

With this purpose in view it will be supposed that three candidates are to be elected from a district and that " each voter may cast as many votes for one candidate as there are representatives to be elected, or may distribute the same or equal parts thereof among the candidates as he shall see fit," as provided in the Constitution of the State of Illinois. For purposes of illustration it will be assumed that we have a district in which say the Republicans are in a minority. In that event they would nominate and run only one candidate, and if the party is well disciplined each voter would cast all his votes for this candidate, who will be designated as A. If the Republicans were sure of a majority of voters in the district they would then know that they could elect two candidates, say A and B, and the voters would all be instructed to give $1\frac{1}{2}$ votes to each of them. If they had three-fourths of the votes then they could elect all three candidates, and under effective party management all the electors would be instructed to give one vote to each of three candidates, *A*, *B* and *C*. It will be seen then that a voter can vote in any of the three following ways :

FIRST.	SECOND.	THIRD.
A—3 votes.	A—1 ½ votes.	A—1 vote.
	B—1 ½ votes.	B—1 vote.
		C—1 vote.

It has been assumed that in determining how to vote he is to a certain extent sure of the number of votes which will be cast for the Republican candidate. This would, however, seldom be the case. There would always be more or less uncertainty whether his party can elect one, two or three candidates. It would therefore be desirable that in case all his votes are needed to elect the candidate whom he prefers to any of the others, or his first choice, that they should all be counted for that one. If, however, two candidates of the party with which the voter is identified can be elected, by dividing all the votes of the party equally between them, then he would ordinarily desire that his votes be so apportioned between the two, whom he or his party would select in preference to a third. If three candidates could be elected by an equal division of the votes among them then the voter would naturally give one vote to each of three.

The voter in other words, should have " the power of expressing his approbation of a considerable number of candidates, by naming them as successors to his vote, without damaging the chances of those who stand highest in his preference."* In other words he should be able to express by his vote in substance this :   " I prefer *A*, the candidate whose name I have placed or marked first on my voting paper or ticket, who is my first choice ; and if they are needed for his election all my votes are to be counted for him. If there are a sufficient number of persons belonging to my party, or holding the same opinions or having the same interests as mine, and who vote as I do, to elect two candidates in this district, then I want my votes to be equally divided between *A* and *B*, the latter being my second choice, and his name is placed or marked second on my ticket. If there are a sufficient number of voters

---

*From a Report of the Committee appointed by the Conference of members of the Reform League of England and others on Mr. Hare's scheme of representation, held 28th February, and 7th and 21st of March, 1868.

who vote as I do to elect three candidates then C is my third choice and is so indicated in my ticket and my votes are to be divided equally between A, B and C."

To fulfill these requirements a system of voting must have what engineers and mechanics call *automatic action*.   It must have an inherent power of adaptation to the condition which may exist at any election and effect a distribution of votes among all the parties and interests that may manifest themselves in the ratio of their numerical strength.   This should be effected too with the smallest possible sacrifice of the elector's personal liberty of choice.

This it is thought can be accomplished by adopting a very simple way of counting cumulative votes, similar to that proposed by Dr. Gustav Burnitz and Dr. George Varrentrapp in a pamphlet * published in Frankfort on the Main in 1863.   A translation of this pamphlet is published in appendix B in this volume, to which the reader is referred. Without considering in detail the theories and methods contained in that pamphlet, the principle proposed by its authors may be illustrated by applying it to the vote of the hypothetical elector, the possible distribution of whose votes was printed in tabular form on page 89.

Assuming that his first choice of the candidates is A, the second B, and the third C, then, as pointed out, his votes may be given in either of the three ways indicated in the table.   If all of them are given to one candidate then they should of course all three be counted for him ; if they are divided equally between two candidates then, obviously, his second choice would get only *half* of the voter's votes.   In fact if he votes for a *second choice* candidate, it implies that he has divided his three votes between two candidates, and therefore *a second choice candidate cannot receive more than half as many votes as one who is a first choice*.   If the votes are distributed equally among three candidates, then the third could get only *one third* of the elector's votes.   It is therefore obvious that a third choice candidate cannot get more than *a third* as many votes as one who is first on the list.

Supposing though, that instead of one Republican voter, that there are a thousand, all of whom have the same preferences as our

---

* " A Method of Assuring to the Majority as well as the Minorities, at all Kinds of Elections, the Number of Representatives Corresponding to their Strength."

hypothetical elector has,—that is, the first choice candidate of all of them is *A*, their second *B*, and their third *C*. It is plain that if they all give their three votes to *A*, that he will have 3000, but if they divide them equally between their first choice candidate *A*, and a second choice *B*, then *B* could only get 1500, or half as many votes as *A* could get if they were all given to him. In other words, on this system, *a second choice candidate can get only half as many votes as a first choice would receive if they are all concentrated on him.* If the votes are divided among three candidates then it is also obvious that *the third can get only one-third as many as the first may have if the voters should plump for him.*

As each of the 1000 voters has three votes, the total number is 3000 which may all be given to the first choice candidate if the whole of them are needed to elect him. If they are divided equally between two candidates then the second choice cannot get more than 1500, or *half* as many as the first, and if divided among three the third will get only 1000, or *one-third* as many as the first.

To determine the maximum number of votes therefore which each candidate can have, *all first choice votes should be divided by 1, all second choice by 2, all third by 3.* This is the fundamental principle underlying Drs. Burnitz and Varrentrapp's system, the simplicity of which will recommend it.

Let it be supposed further that the Democrats also nominate three candidates, *D*, *E* and *F*, and that they have 1200 voters who can cast 3600 votes and that the preference of these voters is expressed in the order in which the candidates are named, that is, *D* is their first choice, *E* the second and *F* the third. Then obviously the greatest number of votes which *D* could get would be 3600, *E* could get 1800 and *F* 1200. Arrange these figures in tabular form and they will be as follows:

REPUBLICAN.	DEMOCRATIC.
1st choice, A, 3,000 votes.	D, 3,600 votes.
2d " B, 1,500 "	E, 1,800 "
3d " C, 1,000 "	F, 1,200 "

As " the three candidates highest in votes shall be declared elected " it is plain that *A*, *D* and *E* will have the highest number in whatever way the votes can be counted. If they are needed to elect the first choice candidates 3000 votes can be counted for A and if they are required to elect D he has 3600 to elect him. If the votes are equally divided between the first and two second choice Republican candidates A and B, then B will have only half as many as A, or 1500, while if the Democratic votes are divided equally between D and E, E would then have 1800 or half as many as D. The vote would therefore be as follows :

A—3,000 votes.   D—1,800 votes.

E—1,800 " "

No other division of the votes can give any of the candidates more than E has if the Democratic votes are equally divided between D and E. Obviously then A, D and E are elected.

The principle which underlies this division of votes and which has been explained, is that if a voter divides his votes equally between two candidates he can give only half as many for his second choice candidate as he could for one alone, and if he divides his votes equally between three he can give only one-third of them to his third choice— in other words, second choice votes count for only half as much as first choices do, and third choice votes for only one-third as much as those for first choices. Without elucidating the subject any further now we may deduce the following very simple rule or law for this method of free voting which for the sake of explicitness will be called the Burnitz system which is applicable to the election of any number of representatives in Congress, state legislatures or municipal or any other legislative or corporate bodies or associations.

RULE FOR VOTING.

Each voter may give on his ballot, the names of not exceeding——* candidates for whom he votes, and may indicate his preferences for such candidates by ordinal numbers marked opposite their names ; or, in the absence of such numbers, the order in which the names are inscribed on his ticket shall indicate the order of his preference, and as many votes shall be counted for each name as there are candidates to be elected.

It will be seen that this rule does not require the voter to do any-

---

* The number to be elected, which, in this example, is three.

thing which he is not obliged to do under the present system of voting. He is now compelled to have the name of a candidate whom he prefers written or printed on his ticket. That is all that is required in the proposed plan. It is true that under the new system a voter has the privilege of voting for more than one candidate if he chooses, but he need not exercise that privilege unless he wishes to do so. If he does vote for more than one, his preference or choice will be implied by the order in which the names of the candidate are arranged.

If this method of voting was adopted it is probable that the different parties would then, as now, have tickets printed and would arrange the names in some order which would comply with the views of the party managers. This arrangement the voter could accept if he likes it, but if the arrangement adopted by the party is not satisfactory to him he could change it by simply writing a number opposite the name of each or any candidate. The candidates names on the tickets might or would be printed somewhat as follows:

Choice	FOR ASSEMBLY.
	Henry Gladstone.
	Dennis O'Connor.
	Julius Bismarck.

Voted in this way it would mean that Gladstone was the voter's first choice, O'Connor his second, and Bismarck his third. If this order was not in accordance with the preference of the voter he might take a pencil or a pen and mark 1 opposite his first choice, which it will be assumed is O'Connor, 2 opposite his second choice which might be Bismarck, and 3 opposite his third choice, so that his ticket would then be as follows:

Choice	FOR ASSEMBLY.
3d	Henry Gladstone.
1st	Dennis O'Connor.
2d	Julius Bismarck.

Now at the risk of repeating what has already been said the reader will be asked to observe :

1. The voter need not vote for more than one candidate unless he chooses to do so.

2. He can vote for as many as he likes not exceeding the number to be elected.

3. He need not indicate his preferences if he has none, or does not want to do it.

4. If the order in which the names are inscribed on the ticket does not represent his preferences, he can change it by simply placing a number opposite to any or all the names.

5. He can put a paster over any of the names or erase it if he does not want to vote it or desires to substitute some other name.

Surely any voter who can exercise the franchise now could do so if this method of free voting was adopted, for the obvious reason that he would not be required to do anything then which he is not doing now when he avails himself of the glorious privilege of taking part in the government of our country.

But it will be said that if a voter is permitted to divide his votes among as many candidates as he chooses, the difficulty will be not in *casting* but in *counting* the votes.   Let us see what this difficulty will be.

In the first place under the proposed system the inspectors and registers of election must count and record how many first, how many second, and how many third choice votes are cast for each candidate.   This, of course, implies some little extra labor and a little additional time.   To do this when the polls are closed, the ballots can be assorted first according to the *first choice votes*—that is, it may be assumed, all those on which *A* is the first choice are sorted together in a pile, then those on which *B* is the first choice, and those of *C*, *D*, *E* and *F*, and the ballots in each pile are then counted and the number of first choice votes for each candidate are entered in a blank somewhat like the following :

RETURN OF VOTES CAST IN THE ——— ELECTION DISTRICT.

Choice.	CANDIDATES.					
	A	B	C	D	E	F
1st						
2d						
3d						

When this is done the ballots are reassorted according to the second choice, counted and entered, and afterwards the process would be repeated for the third choice. When the votes cast are entered in the blank it would appear somewhat like that shown below. This,

RETURN OF VOTES CAST IN THE FIRST ELECTION DISTRICT.

Choice.	CANDIDATES.					
	A	B	C	D	E	F
1st	2750	201	49	3333	166	101
2d	189	2726	85	184	3274	142
3d	108	285	2607	97	374	3129

or a copy of it, would then be sent to the district canvasser or board or other authority appointed for making the final count of the district, who would enter the returns on a blank somewhat like that on page 96, in which the number of the election district would be entered in the first column, the number of 1st, 2d and 3d choice votes cast for *A* would be entered on the same horizontal line, as the number of the district, and in the appropriate columns below the candidates' names, where the returns belong, as indicated by the headings. The same would be done with the votes for the other candidates, and the re-

ELECTION RETURNS FROM .... ASSEMBLY DISTRICT OF THE STATE OF NEW YORK.

ELECTION DISTRICTS.	A			B			C			D			E			F		
	1st choice votes.	2d choice votes.	3d choice votes	1st choice votes.	2d choice votes	3d choice votes	1st choice votes.	2d choice votes.	3d choice votes.	1st choice votes.	2d choice votes.	3d choice votes	1st choice votes.	2d choice votes.	3d choice votes	1st choice votes.	2d choice votes.	3d choice votes.
First........	2750	189	108	201	2726	285	49	85	2607	3333	184	97	166	3274	374	101	142	3129
Second........																		
Third........																		
Fourth........																		
Fifth........																		
Sixth........																		
Seventh........																		
Eighth........																		
Ninth........																		
Tenth........																		
Twelfth........																		
Thirteenth........																		
Fourteenth........																		
Total........																		

CANDIDATES.

turns from all the other election districts.   When the returns from all
the districts are entered the votes in each vertical column would be
added up, which gives the total number of 1st, 2d and 3d choice votes
cast for each candidate in the whole assembly or other district.

Now to count these votes in accordance with the principles which
have been explained the following rule has been formulated :

RULE FOR COUNTING THE VOTES.

*The first, second and third preference votes for the different candidates
shall each be counted separately; the total number of first preferences,
for each candidate, shall be divided by 1, the second preferences by 2 and
the third by 3.   The quotients thus obtained for each candidate shall be
added together and their sum will be his elective quotient.   The three
candidates having the highest elective quotients shall be declared elected.*

To make the final determination or summation of the votes a blank
somewhat like that shown on page 98 could be used. The sums from
the returns in the table like that on page 96 would be carried to the appropriate column in the table on page 98.   Next to the column headed
" votes" is another headed " quotients."   Then in accordance with the
rule for counting, the first choice votes for each candidate are divided
by 1, and the quotient is carried into the adjoining column headed "quotients" or what is the same thing the entire number of first choice votes is
carried into this column.   The second choice votes are then divided by ·
two and the quotients carried into the column of quotients, and the
third choice votes are divided by three and the quotients are transferred
to column of quotients.   In the table on page 98 such division has been
made with imaginary figures.   When this has been done for the votes
of all the candidates the columns of "quotients" are added up and
the sums are the *"elective quotients"* and "the three candidates having the highest elective quotients shall be declared elected."   Striking
out the lowest election quotients until three only are left makes it
obvious that *A*, *D* and *E* are elected.

Considerable objection has been made to cumulative voting on
account of the difficulty of counting fractional votes which must be
employed if voters are permitted to divide their votes equally among
different candidates.   In Illinois voters can divide their votes into

SUMMATION OF VOTES FOR ASSEMBLYMEN IN ——— DISTRICT OF THE STATE OF NEW YORK.

	A		B		C		D		E		F	
CANDIDATES.	Votes.	Quotients	Votes.	Quotients	Votes.	Quotients	Votes.	Quotients	Votes	Quotients	Votes.	Quotients
1st Choice..........	68750	68750	5025	5025	1225	1225	83325	83325	4150	4150	2525	2525
2d Choice..........	4725	2362½	68150	34075	2125	1062½	4600	2300	81850	40925	3550	1775
3d Choice..........	2700	900	7125	2375	65175	21725	2415	805	9350	3116⅔	78225	26075
Elective Quotients....		72012⅙		41475		24012½		86430		48191⅔		30375

halves. A few of the respondents to the circular of inquiry on this subject say there is sometimes difficulty in counting fractional votes of as little vulgarity as a ½. If more than three candidates should be elected from a district it would be necessary to add up halves, thirds, quarters, fifths and perhaps other fractions still more vulgar. That ignorant inspectors and registers of election might find difficulty in doing this is quite probable. Especial attention is called to the fact that with the system which is proposed here inspectors have no other duty to perform than to count and record the votes cast in the district. They must count three classes of votes for each candidate instead of one—when three are elected. This is the *only* addition to the amount or the complexity of their work.

Neither are the duties of the district canvassers increased in complexity further than to require that the 1st, 2d and 3d votes cast for each candidate shall be divided by 1, 2 and 3 respectively. Other than this, the only mathematical qualification required for the performance of their duties is the ability to add up columns of figures representing the votes cast and that intellectual equipment they must have now. The fractional votes which are so much dreaded by some do not appear at all excepting perhaps as final quantities in the quotients when the total votes are not susceptible of equal division by the ordinal numbers which represent the preferences of voters. It should be observed :

1. That the voter need not do anything which he is not required to do now.

2. All that the inspectors of election, poll and ballot clerks in the local districts must do which is not required of them at present is to *count* and *record* several classes of votes for each candidate, instead of one class for one candidate.

3. The complexity of the general district canvassers duties and the amount of work which they must do are increased only by the requirement of recording and summing up three classes of votes for each candidate, instead of one class for each and dividing the sums by 1, 2 and 3, and summing up the quotients.

There is nothing in the proposed method of voting which requires any additional mental effort greater than the voter must now exert. If there be anything which affords a pretense of foundation for the charge of complexity, it is the appropriation of the votes after the ballot or polling is over ; and this is to be performed by properly instructed and responsible officers, under careful and scrupulous control, and subject to the critical inspection of the parties especially concerned. But even if there is some slight addition to the duties of the officers of elections and to the complexity of the methods of counting the votes it may be answered that "the object of government is *justice* and not simplicity."

But those to whom this improved system is proposed may very properly ask what advantages will it have over the Illinois method of cumulative voting ?

To this it may be answered that it will obviate entirely that practical difficulty pointed out by the correspondent from Joliet which is that "a voter cannot tell when he is casting more votes than a favorite candidate needs." It will remove entirely the motive and inducement for "plumping" when there is no need for it and the evils which result therefrom and which have been indicated by some of the respondents to the inquiries which have been made concerning the working of the Illinois system. It will give to each or any party a number of representatives proportionate to its votes and make it unnecessary for the party managers or the voters to estimate the strength of their party in order to determine how many votes to cast for respective candidates. It would in effect say to voters,—"you can select the candidate who is your first preference and cast your vote for him. If all your votes are required to elect your first choice they will all be counted for him. If, however, there are enough votes cast for the candidates both of your first and second choice then *your* votes will be divided between those two or if it is possible to elect the three preferred by you then your votes will be divided equally between those three." The system is "automatic" and adapts itself perfectly to the varying strength of parties and to the wishes, intentions and preferences of voters and gives them the utmost freedom in assigning their votes to whoever will represent their views and interests most satisfactorily. It enables the voter at the polls to declare in substance this—which has been expressed before—"If required to elect the candidate whom I have indicated as my first choice I hereby direct that all my votes be given to him if they are needed to elect him. If there are a sufficient number of votes cast for him and for the candidate I have designated as my second preference then I direct that my votes be divided equally between the two. If enough votes are cast to elect both of these candidates and the one whose name I have selected as my third choice then my votes are to be divided equally between all three.

This system is equally well adapted to the election of a larger number of representatives than three as it is to that number, and its advantages become more marked when the number is increased as will be shown farther on.

CHAPTER IX.

Notwithstanding the fact, as ' was said by a writer in the *Nation*, " that when properly stated, the correctness of the principle of minority representation forces admission," and that the principle has been before the world and has been earnestly discussed and advocated by some of the ablest minds in Europe and this country, it must be, admitted that, nevertheless, it has made comparatively little advance. The adoption of cumulative voting in Illinois, nearly twenty-five years ago, and the election of members of the legislature in that state · ever since by that system, its application to the election of school boards in England, and of the members of the governing bodies in some cities and corporations here, the adoption of the principle of pro- portional representation in Denmark and some of the cantons of Switzerland, is about all the advance that has been made.

As long ago as September, 1886, the editor of the *Nation* began an article in that paper with the remark that "For several years past the question of ' personal,' or ' proportional,' or ' minority' representation, which at one time attracted a good deal of attention, has been tacitly dropped out of sight." One of the reasons given for the disappearance of the subject from public discussions was that " the reform of the civil service was more imperative, and the cham- pions of reform in administrative methods wisely concentrated all their efforts for the time upon the one principal issue. But," this writer continues, "the chief reason for the loss of interest in it was undoubtedly *the want of any thoroughly satisfactory scheme of propor- tional representation.*"

Most persons who are at all familiar with the subject, and the dis- cussion of it, during the past twenty-five years or more, will, it is thought, agree that this reason for the loss of interest in the subject is probably the true one.

One of the purposes of this compilation has been to show the results and the advantages and disadvantages of the system of electing representatives by cumulative voting in the State of Illinois. It is thought that the evidence submitted has shown that a distinct gain in the promotion of good government has resulted there from that method of election although the experience of more than twenty years has shown some serious defects in it, which have been pointed out and are now recognized. Cumulative voting is therefore not a "thoroughly satisfactory scheme," although in justice to the advocates of minority representation, it should be said that the defects of the Illinois system were anticipated at the time, or very soon after it was adopted. In view of this experience, and of the fact that nowhere in the world has there been any general adoption of the principles of minority representation, notwithstanding that it has been advocated by some of the most eminent public men in this and in European countries, those in whose minds the justice and righteousness of its principles have "forced admission," may be expected to have an answer to the question whether now, after twenty or thirty years, or more, of discussion and experience with various systems of cumulative and other kinds of voting, there is any one which in the words of the writer in the *Nation*, is "thoroughly satisfactory." It is true that such a demand seems somewhat inordinate. The adoption of minority representation in our elections implies a peaceful revolution in the methods by which power is conferred on those who are to govern us. To expect that a scheme which would be thoroughly satisfactory would be evolved by comparatively a few years' experience, is to expect a result seldom attained in methods of government. A scheme which is satisfactory to the extent only of being an advance over the old method of elections of single members in each district, by a majority of the voters, —and this may rightly be claimed for cumulative voting—is about all that can be reasonably expected at the present juncture.

It remains to show that the system of voting and of assigning and counting votes, which has been explained, will overcome the difficulty which voters would encounter under the cumulative plan, of knowing how many candidates to vote for and of dividing their votes equally among them, and of counting the votes, if the districts are enlarged and the number of members to be elected from each is increased.

To do this it will be supposed that A, B, C, D and E are candidates of one party in a district where five members are to be elected. A voter, if he divides his votes equally among different numbers of candidates could distribute them in any of the five following ways :

1	2	3	4	5
A, 5 votes.	A, 2½ votes.	A, 1⅔ votes.	A, 1¼ votes,	A, 1 vote.
	B, 2½ "	B, 1⅔ "	B, 1¼ "	B, 1 "
		C, 1⅔ "	C, 1¼ "	C, 1 "
			D, 1¼ "	D, 1 "
				E, 1 "

If there were seven candidates then the votes could be divided in the following seven different ways :

1	2	3	4	5	6	7
A, 7 vt.	A, 3½ vt.	A, 2⅓ vt.	A, 1¾ vt.	A, 1⅖ vt.	A, 1⅙ vt.	A. 1 vt.
	B, 3½ "	B, 2⅓ "	B, 1¾ "	B, 1⅖ "	B, 1⅙ "	B, 1 "
		C, 2⅓ "	C, 1¾ "	C, 1⅖ "	C, 1⅙ "	C, 1 "
			D, 1¾ "	D, 1⅖ "	D, 1⅙ "	D, 1 "
				E, 1⅖ "	E, 1⅙ "	E, 1 "
					F, 1⅙ "	F, 1 "
						G, 1 "

It can readily be seen how great the difficulty would be for electors and for parties which influence or control them, to know how under such conditions to distribute their votes. Besides this perplexity there is also the ignorant voter and stupid election inspector and poll clerk whose incapacity must be considered. It would probably be quite beyond the mathematical attainments of even average voters to divide five votes equally between three or four candidates, and to distribute seven equally among three, four, five or six would drive them to distraction, or the inaction of non-voting. Then in the counting of votes it is very doubtful whether ordinary inspectors of election and ballot clerks would be able to add up correctly columns of figures including halves, thirds and quarters, and if complicated with fifths and sixths it would be hopeless to expect correct results.

It has been explained that in three member districts a voter is not required by the proposed system of voting to vote or make up his ballot any differently than he must at present. That is, he can vote for a single candidate in exactly the same way as he does now, but he has the privilege of voting for more than one, not exceeding the whole number to be elected if he chooses to avail himself of that privilege. His preferences for the different candidates may be indicated by the order in which the names are arranged on his ticket. If this order does not accord with his preferences it is provided that he can change it by simply inscribing ordinal numbers opposite the names of the candidates. It is repeated that the voter need not do anything more in voting than he does now but he has the additional privileges which have been explained. Now in applying this method to the election of five or seven, or any number of representatives, the principle and the practice so far as the voter is concerned is identical to that employed in electing three members excepting that he has the privilege of voting for more candidates, that is, as many as there are members to be elected, and can indicate his preferences in the same way as before. An illustration of its application to a five member district may make this a little clearer.

To do this it will be supposed that each of the dominant parties, the Democratic and Republican, nominate as many candidates as there are members to be elected; and that the following represent the respective tickets of the two parties:

REPUBLICAN TICKET.

Choice.	FOR ASSEMBLY.
	James Allen.
	David Foster.
	Alexander Pratt.
	Robert Booth.
	Lyman Wheeler.

DEMOCRATIC TICKET.

Choice.	FOR. ASSEMBLY.
3	Frank Campbell.
2	Josiah Weeks.
4	Allen Bush.
1	Dennis Flannigan.
5	Aaron Goldberg.

These would be printed as they now are under the existing laws, and regulations prevailing in the different states. If a Republican voter was satisfied with the ticket as printed and provided by his party managers, he would vote it just as it is represented. By doing so he would be declaring his preference for the candidate—James Allen—named first in the list, who would be his first choice. His second choice would be the one—David Foster—who stands next on the list, and his third choice would be Alexander Pratt, and so on. But supposing that a voter was not satisfied with the order of preference in which the candidates are named—for instance, if the first choice of a Democratic voter was not Frank Campbell but Dennis Flannigan, in order to express this preference in his vote all he would be obliged to do would be to inscribe a figure 1 in front of Flannigan's name as shown. If Josiah Weeks was his second choice he would mark his name accordingly, and would also mark the other candidates in the order of his preference as shown. As remarked before, there is nothing in the proposed method of voting which requires any mental effort greater than that which a voter must exert at present.

Let it be supposed though that the independent Democrats in the district are dissatisfied with the ticket nominated by the regulars, and that they think they can elect a candidate who will represent them more acceptably. They therefore conclude to nominate a ticket of their own, but are uncertain whether they can elect more than one candidate, and being reasonably well satisfied with the third of the regular Democratic nominees, they conclude to make him the second candidate on a ticket headed by Thomas Tiffany, an "anti snapper," we will assume.

This ticket would then be as follows :

INDEPENDENT DEMOCRATIC TICKET.

Choice.	FOR ASSEMBLY.
	Thomas Tiffany.
	Allen Bush.

Each voter can now vote one of the regular tickets if he chooses to do so, or he can scratch out any name he likes, or if they are not arranged in the order of his choice he can change it by placing an ordinal number opposite any name which will designate which candidate is his 1st, 2d, 3d, 4th or 5th choice, as has been explained. In other words he has the utmost liberty in voting. If he chooses he can vote for one candidate, just as he does now, or for two, three, four or five. If the names have been inscribed by the party managers in the regularly printed tickets in the order of the voter's preference, he votes it as printed. If their order is not in accordance with his preferences, he indicates the latter by marking ordinal numbers opposite the names which will express it. He is not obliged, as in Illinois, to indicate on his ticket how many votes he will give to each candidate. What he expresses in effect is—"I will give all my votes to my favorite candidate, who is my first choice, if they are needed to elect him, or I will divide them between as many of my two, three or more favorites as can be elected." Whether they can be will be determined by the counting of the votes.

The independents it will be supposed are in revolt. The regular Democrats have—as they often do—placed an unfit and unsatisfactory candidate at the head of their ticket, which determines some of the voters to make an independent nomination, and run an independent ticket. They select Thomas Tiffany, a man, it will be assumed, of marked ability and integrity and with the qualifications demanded by the independents to represent their views and interests—and place him at the head of their ticket.   They then agree by a canvass of the district to vote for him as their 1st choice.

The counting and return of the votes to the district canvassers from the different election districts would then be exactly the same as has been already described and made in a blank similar to that on page 95, excepting that there would be the names of more candidates on it.   These returns would be entered on a blank similar to the one on page 96, but with columns for 1st, 2d, 3d, 4th and 5th choice votes instead of three only.   When all the returns are received and tabulated and the votes in each column are added up the sums at the foot of the columns would be carried to the appropriate places in a blank similar to the one on page 98, but with five horizontal lines for the five classes of votes. The sums thus entered in this blank are then divided by the ordinal numbers and the quotients carried into the columns with that heading.   It is assumed that the figures in the last blank represent the results of an election in a district in which three members are to be elected.   The quotients for each candidate are then added up, and the lowest one is crossed out.   This operation is continued until only five quotients, which are the highest, are left.   The candidates for whom these were cast, being "the highest in votes," are elected.

This system can be applied to the election of seven, nine or any number of representatives from a district and will always give a representation proportioned to the number of any body of electors who may vote for the same candidate or candidates.

In order to make the practice which exists in Illinois and the system which has been explained here more nearly parallel, it has been assumed in the explanation of the latter that when three members are to be elected, that each voter can give three votes for each candidate, but in the final count those cast for the second choice candidate are to be divided by 2 and those for the third choice by 3.   To carry out this parallel, if five members are to be elected then each voter should be allowed to give five votes for each, those for the second, third, fourth and fifth choice candidates to be divided by 2, 3, 4, and 5, as has been explained.

It does not matter so far as the result is concerned whether each voter gives five votes to each candidate or whether he gives one to each, which may be divided into five parts. It is only a difference in the method of expressing and representing the fact that the voter has a certain amount of voting power or potency, all of which may be given to one candidate, or a half to another, or a third to another, and so on. It is a mere verbal distinction to call the voting power which an elector can give to one candidate five votes, or to call it one vote divided into five parts. As there undoubtedly is more or less popular prejudice against allowing a voter to cast more than one vote for a single candidate, it would seem to be better if "a system of free voting is adopted" to call each person's voting power one vote, and permit it to be divided and distributed in equal parts thereof among different candidates. As explained this would not affect the final result in any way.

Owing to the prejudice referred to, it therefore seems in every way desirable that the votes of electors should be limited to one for each of as many candidates as he chooses to vote for, not exceeding the number to be elected in the general district. It is therefore recommended that each voter simply give the names of the candidates he prefers in his ballot and that one vote be counted for each, the votes to be subject to the division in the final count, which has been explained.

The number of representatives elected in each district should however always be an odd one, that is three, five or seven and not four, six or eight. The reason for this may perhaps be made plain easiest by an illustration. Let it be supposed that the Democrats in a district have 36,360 voters and the Republicans 48,470, and that six members are to be elected. If each of the two parties runs three candidates and all the voters cast one* vote for each candidate, in the manner which has been explained and recommended, then on the final division and count, the result would be as follows :

---

* In practice there would of course be more or less scattering of votes, that is, some voters would select one candidate for their first, second third, etc., choices and some would choose others ; it is not likely that all would vote in the same way as has been indicated in the table for the purposes of this illustration.

DEMOCRATS.

CHOICE.	A Votes.	A Quotient	B Votes.	B Quotient	C Votes.	C Quotient	D Votes.	D Quotient	E Votes.	E Quotient	F Votes.	F Quotient
1st	36,360	36,360										
2d			36,360	18,180								
3d					36,360	12,120						
4th							36,360	9,090				
5th									36,360	7,272		
6th											36,360	6,060
Elective Quotients.....		36,360		18,180		12,120		9,090		7,272		6,060

REPUBLICANS

CHOICE.	G Votes.	G Quotient	H Votes.	H Quotient	I Votes.	I Quotient	J Votes.	J Quotient	K Votes.	K Quotient	L Votes.	L Quotient
1st	48,470	48,470										
2d			48,470	24,235								
3d					48,470	16,156⅔						
4th							48,470	12,117¾				
5th									48,470	9,694		
6th											48,470	8,078¾
Elective Quotients.		48,470		24,235		16,156⅔				9,694		8,078

Striking out the lowest elective quotients beginning with 6060 and successively 7272, 8078½, 9090, 9694 and 12,117½ until there are only six such quotients left and it will be seen that A, B and C, on the Democratic ticket and G, H and I on the Republican would be elected. That is the Republicans with only 36,360 votes will elect as many representatives as the Democrats do with with 48,470. A little analysis will show that if six members are elected *"unless the party in a majority exceeds the minority, in a proportion of more than four to three, it cannot secure a majority of members, when both parties make the best use of their numbers,"** and three members of each party would be elected in the preceding example in spite of the fact that the Republicans had a majority of 12,110.

If there is any one political maxim more firmly rooted in the American mind than another it is the one which asserts that "the majority should rule." As has been said "popular opinion has elevated it to the sanctity of a great principle of free government." A system of election which would withhold from majorities power which it is thought rightfully belongs to them would be certain to encounter great public opposition and excite great dissatisfaction, and would not be tolerated for any great length of time. If however five or seven or any other odd number of members were elected from each district by the method which has been explained, then whichever party has a majority of voters can always elect a majority of the representatives. Thus with the figures which have been used for the preceding illustration, if only five candidates were to be elected then C would have been defeated and the Democrats would have elected two and the Republicans three. If seven members were elected then J would have had to be counted in and the Republicans would have had three and the Democrats four. This same result would be reached if the Democrats had a majority of only one. In other words if an odd number of candidates are elected from each district, then, if there are two parties nearly equally divided the one having a bare majority of the voters can always elect a majority of the representatives; which accords with the traditional rights of majorities. It is

---

*G. Shaw Lefevre, in *Nineteenth Century*, of May, 1884.

true that if a third party should run a candidate in a district in which an odd number of representatives is· to be elected, it might produce the same condition of things between the first and second parties that would exist if an even number of candidates were elected in the district by two parties alone, but in that event, the result would be due and would be attributed to the action of the third party and it would not be a result inherent in the system of election. In times of great political excitement, to withhold from the party which has a decided majority of the voters, the advantage accruing from having a majority of the representatives, would be certain to produce great public hostility from them which might lead to very serious results.

The modification of the Burnitz system for electing representatives to national, state, municipal and corporate bodies may then be summarily described as follows :

1st. An odd number of representatives greater than two should be elected in each district.

2d. Each voter may give on his ballot the names of not exceeding ——* *candidates for whom he votes, and may indicate his preferences for such candidates by ordinal numbers marked opposite their names ; or, in the absence of such numbers, the order in which the names are inscribed on his ticket shall indicate the order of his preferences.*

3d. The first, second, third, fourth, etc., preference names for the different candidates to be counted separately ; the total number of first preferences of each candidate to be divided by one, the second preferences by two, the third by three, and so on. The quotients thus obtained for each candidate to be added together, and their sum will be his elective quotient. The number of candidates who are to be elected having the highest elective quotients shall be declared elected.

This system is applicable to and is adapted for any kind of elections in which any number of members greater than two are to be elected. It is as well suited to the election of presidential electors and members of Congress as it is to state legislatures, and representatives in municipal governing bodies, primary meetings, corporate or other associations. It is believed that if it is adopted any number of

---

*The number to be elected.

members may be elected in a district without encountering any of the difficulties which have been experienced with cumulative voting. Its advantages may then be finally summed up as follows:

1st. It will give perfect freedom to the voter in the selection of candidates and the concentration of his votes, and will give them their full efficacy. No additional mental or physical effort greater than that which is demanded by the present method of voting will be required of him, either antecedent to or during the act of casting his ballot.

2d. No other duties are demanded of inspectors of election, poll and ballot clerks, than are required now, excepting to count and record several classes of votes, for each candidate, instead of one only.

3d. The general district canvassers will be required, as now, to record and sum up the votes reported from the local districts, to divide the sums by their ordinal numbers and then sum up the quotients. The only additions to their duties are those resulting from the increase in the number of ordinal *classes* of votes or preferences for candidates, the division of the sums of their votes by their ordinal numbers, and the final summation of the quotients, which are all very simple processes.

"If," as was said of the Hare system, "there be anything which affords a pretense of foundation for the charge of complexity, it is the appropriations of the votes after the ballot or polling is over; and this is to be performed by properly instructed and responsible officers, under careful and scrupulous control, and subject to the critical inspection of the parties especially concerned." Surely a charge that the proposed system is complex has little basis to rest on, and even if it had the response might again be made that " the object of government is justice and not simplicity." We have it on the authority of the modern philosophers that " all organic development is a change from a state of homogeneity to a state of heterogeneity." Political evolution is a like process.

In order to formulate the general principles of the Burnitz system of election into a concrete form the following amendment to the Constitution of the State of New York has been framed. It is based on the one proposed by the Proportional Representation Society of New York, which contains a provision for the election of state senators and assemblymen and members of the legislative bodies of cities by a system of cumulative voting. The following amendment is intended as a substitute for some of the provisions of Article III. of the present Constitution :

ARTICLE III.

SECTION 1.   The legislative power of this State shall be vested in a Senate and Assembly.

SEC. 2.   The Senate shall consist of thirty-five members, and the Assembly of one hundred and forty members.   The Senators and the Assemblymen shall be chosen for two years.

SEC. 3.   The Legislature, at its first session, after this article shall have become part of the Constitution, shall divide the State into five Senate districts, and declare the boundaries thereof ; and shall also divide the State into twenty Assembly districts and declare the boundaries thereof.

SEC. 4.   The Senate and Assembly districst shall consist of convenient and contiguous territory, shall have a population, excluding aliens, as nearly equal as may be conveniently practicable and not less than seven Senators and seven Assemblymen shall be elected from each district at the same time.

SEC. 5.   And to insure a real freedom of voting for and of election of Senators and Assemblymen, each qualified voter in each of these districts may give on his ballot the names of not exceeding seven candidates for the Senate and Assembly respectively, for whom he votes ; and may indicate his preferences for such candidates by ordinal numbers marked opposite their names ; or, in the absence of such numbers the order in which the names are inscribed on his ballot shall indicate the order of his preferences.

SEC. 6.   After the closing of the polls on the day of election, the canvass in each election district shall be completed by ascertaining and counting, separately, and making returns to a Board of District Canvassers, in the respective Senate and Assembly districts, of the number of the first, second, third, etc., votes given for each candidate. From the returns so made the Boards of District Canvassers in each district shall determine the total number each of first, second, third, etc., preference votes cast for each candidate in the respective districts.   The total number of first preference votes for each candidate shall then be divided by 1, the total number of second preference votes by 2, the third by 3 and so on.   The quotients thus obtained for each candidate shall be added together and their sum will be his *elective quotient*. The seven candidates for the Senate and Assembly having the highest elective quotients in the respective districts shall be declared elected.

SEC. 7.   If a member of the Senate or Assembly shall die or resign, or his seat become vacant for any reason, the remainder of his term shall be served by the candidate who had the next highest elective quotient of the body of electors to which such member belongs.

SEC. 8. The Legislature shall also enact a law requiring the several cities of the state to be divided into districts for the election of the members of their respective legislative bodies, which election shall be according to such method of free voting and election, described in Sections 5 and 6 of this article.

SEC. 9. Such municipal districts shall have, as nearly as practicable, an equal population, exclusive of aliens. Not less than seven such members shall be elected from each of the districts at the same time.

SEC. 10. In case of a vacancy occurring in any such municipal legislative bodies it shall be filled in the same manner as presented for Senators and Assemblymen in Section 7 of this article.

CHAPTER X.

To show still further some of the political evils from which we are now suffering, and how they could be overcome, by a system of free voting, an illustration will be given. In the city of New York the nomination of candidates for the state legislature and the local board of aldermen is almost absolutely controlled by the professional politicians and party managers in and through their organizations, caucuses and party machinery. We, the voters, are victims of the "machines," and as a practical politician recently said : "It's great sport to see people go to the polls in herds and vote like cattle for the ticket *we prepare.* * * * The people think they make the nominations, but we do that business for them." The candidates thus nominated as some one else has said "represent, not the will of the majority, but the tyranny of an active and unscrupulous minority." If he had said of two or more minorities who give us a choice of evils in the candidates they nominate the statement would have been more nearly in accordance with the experience of many voters. Under this tyrannical control of political affairs, as Mr. Sterne has said in his book, from which we have quoted before : "To become one of the dominant majority, the citizen must attach himself to the party in power, or to one which has the opportunity to come into power ; to do so the voter must, in a majority of cases, surrender his individual preferences as to men, and as often to measures, which he believes to be for the public welfare, so that some of his opinions may prevail, or that some tenet of the opposite party, to which he is more especially adverse, may not become law," or what is perhaps still worse for the public welfare "many men, not liking the choice of evils which party machinery presents to their view, prefer to disfranchise themselves rather than become party to the elevation of unfit and improper men to political power. * * * If they belong to the minority in opinion they throw away their votes, as representation is denied to the min-

ority.   If they belong to the majority, they may be compelled
to vote for men who turn uppermost in the machinery of party,
and in whose professions that they will carry out the party principles they have no faith.''   In support of this Mr. Sterne also
quotes what Mr. J. Francis Fisher says in a pamphlet on Reform
in Municipal Elections : '' that, in the progress of years, when
he wished to take his humble part as a constituent unit in the
body politic, he found himself thrust aside from the procession of state
as if he had no legitimate place in its ranks.   At the various elections
he seldom found any candidate presented to him whom he could sin-
cerely approve ; still more rarely one whom he could support with zeal.
He always voted for those he thought the worthiest and generally without
party prejudice, and the result was that he was almost always in the
ranks of the defeated.   Although classed among the educated and
wealthy, he felt himself as much disfranchised as if he had been excluded from the polls by law.   He had no voice in any nomination,
only a selection among those he *would not* have chosen.   Many of his
most valued friends were in the same category, and with him almost
despaired of redress.''   This was written more than twenty-five years
ago and probably it will express with more or less accuracy what many
persons have experienced at nearly every election held during that
period.   It happens often that honest men having the public interest
and good government at heart are disposed to use their influence and
power, whatever it may be to secure the election of worthy representatives. To quote Mr. Sterne again : '' In every electoral district, in every
community, some men will be found with penetration enough to discover the weaknesses, the follies, and the vices of their neighbors, and
who are both skillful and unscrupulous enough to make them subservient to their own ends.''   When the public spirited patriotic
citizen goes out in the service of his city, his state or his country, he
often finds that there is no scarcity of the class of people described by
Mr. Sterne, and he may learn that there is one body of them in league,
if not with the vice, at least with the vicious in the district, and another
apparently antagonistic to the first, but with common interests in
venality and the two are bound together for the protection of those
interests, and ready to condone any of the short-comings or wrong-

doings of their adversaries for the sake of an alliance for the protection of their selfish aims or purposes.

With the exception of Illinois all our states, cities and towns are, for representative purposes, divided into districts, each district having a certain number of inhabitants who have but one representative, who is necessarily elected by a majority of the voters in the district. " The hallucination of this," as Mr. Sterne says, " is, that the right of the majority to govern carries with it the right of the majority to sole representation." In the assembly and aldermanic districts of the city of New York the Democrats generally have decided majorities. There is, nevertheless a very large body of Republican voters scattered over the city who are almost entirely unrepresented in the state legislature and in the board of aldermen. The primaries are in the hands of the politicians who are prone to make such nominations as will best secure their nefarious purposes. From these candidates we, the Democratic, Republican, or independent voters must choose the persons who are to be our representatives. There is no freedom of choice, on the contrary there is constraint and compulsion to vote for men we would not choose to represent us if we were free to make our own selection. The Democrats having a majority of the votes generally elect their candidates, with the result that the large body of Republican and independent voters in New York are unrepresented or are practically disfranchised. Just the reverse of this is true in many of the counties where the Republicans are in a majority.

" Absolute acquiescence in the will of the majority, fairly pronounced," Mr. Buckalew said, " is a vital principle of our system, or one at least, which must be applied and carried out constantly, or our experiment of free government would end in failure. But Mr. Mill long ago pointed out the fact that the majority vote, as heretofore existing in Great Britain and in the United States, does not secure the will of the majority—that, in point of fact, the rule which we get from it, as we apply it is a rule of the majority of the majority, or often of a small portion only of the people. In the first place at the popular elections you count out all the minority voters ; you count or allow only majority votes and put aside the rest. A large part of the people, then, are virtually disfranchised, they have no further voice in the government beyond the giving of fruitless votes, which, after being scored down, are in effect scored out again. Then the representatives so chosen meet in a legislative body, and when any measure of policy is to be voted upon, the majority rule is applied again, and the minority of the legislative body ignored, so that the majority of the legislative body pronounces the rule of law for the citizen.

" Besides, in practice in this country, legislative majorities, upon all measures of a political character at least, and many others, act under a system of consultation—that is, under what we call the caucus rule. The representatives of the majority in the representative body meet together, and subject their wills to the decision of a majority of themselves ; and that caucus decision, concerted and settled in secret, becomes the law of the state. The caucus is in the third degree removed from the people, and there are three eliminations of popular power before the law is enacted. Therefore I say you do not necessarily secure the rule of the majority under your majority vote, because the majority of the legislative body, made up as I have described it, and acting as it does, may very likely represent only a minority of the people out of doors, and such, in point of fact, is frequently the case.''

A great evil, too, in our country is the frequent changes in the membership of our legislative bodies. This was very forcibly stated in the report of a Select Committee on Representative Reform—of which Mr. Buckalew was chairman—submitted to the Senate of the United States in 1869. It was then said :

" It is believed that changes are now too frequent in the House, and that the public interests suffer detriment from this cause. The committee give their unqualified approval to that provision of the constitution which assigns short terms of service to members of the House. But frequency of election does not involve rapidity of change. Popular power may be retained over the House, and yet the great part of its members be continued by reëlection for a considerable period of time ; in other words, frequent elections and permanent membership are not incompatible.

" But, in point of fact, the members of the House are frequently changed so that members of less than four years' service always constitute a large majority, and it is a rare case that a member continues beyond a third term. Under such a system or practice of rapid change, the average character of the House for ability cannot be high. Two and four year men can know but little of the business of govern ment, can be but imperfectly qualified to curb abuses in the executive department, and to expose or comprehend the true character of most questions of domestic and foreign policy.

"There are several reasons which account for frequent change in the membership of the House, of which the single-district system is chief. The fluctuation of party power is next in importance, but is intimately connected with the former. The single-district system has carried the idea of local representation to excess, and has produced a class of inconveniences peculiar to itself. The idea of assigning a representative by law to a special district within a state is naturally supplemented by the idea of rotation in the representative privilege among the localities within the district. Hence, very commonly party nominations are made in turn to the several counties, parishes, or other municipal divisions of the district, which necessitates the frequent selection of new men for representative nomination. The claim of locality becomes more importunate, and is often more regarded than the claims or fitness of candidates in making party nominations, and this although there is no diversity of interest among the people in the different parts of the district. The other cause which we have mentioned coöperates with this, though subordinate to it in effect. Changes of party power in districts where one party does not largely predominate over another, are at all times likely to occur and to defeat the member of the House from the district, although his own party may desire to continue him in the public service. These causes of change would have but slight operation if delegations from states were elected by general ticket, and would have still less if they were selected upon the plan of cumulative or free vote as the practicable and effectual measure of reform. It will continue members of merit for long periods of time in the House, because it will relieve them and those who support them from the causes of change above mentioned. They can be reëlected with certainty so long as the party whose representatives they are desire their continuance in service, and it may be reasonably expected that some men of distinction and intellectual power will always be found in the House whose period of service counts by twenty or thirty years.   They will be the great representatives of the party, and will give lustre and power and usefulness to the House, while they will be the objects of profound attachment and of honest pride in the states they represent.   Congress will become, much more than at present, a theatre of statesmanship and a fit representative of a great people, whose extended territory, diverse populations and varied interests demand great ability and wisdom in the enactment of the laws.   Our present system, admirably calculated to repress merit, will be supplanted by one which will produce precisely the opposite result.

"At present a member of the House holding his seat insecurely cannot devote himself to public business with that zeal and confidence which his position demands   He is involved all the time in a contest for official existence, and his energies are thereby absorbed and wasted. If he has a just ambition to serve the people he must repress rivals at home, must overcome a rule of rotation in his district and fortify himself against fluctuations of party power.   It will be expected of him that he shall distribute the patronage of the government to men who will be efficient in his support for reëlection ; and thus appointments to office and government contracts are to be his peculiar study and their distribution a leading object of his labor.   And he must be liberal in his expenditure of money upon elections to retain his popularity and place ; and the more of political contribution from abroad he can obtain to influence elections in his district the more admired and the more secure he will be.

"In brief, his time and his efforts, instead of being expended for the public, must be expended on personal objects if he desires to remain for any considerable time a representative of the people.   Undoubtedly many of the best men of the country must be deterred from entering upon a congressional career, continuance in which requires such sacrifices to an evil system, so much of unpleasant effort, attended with more uncertainty and probable mortification."

One of the greatest political evils from which we are now suffering is the indifference and apathy which exists among voters with reference to political affairs.   They say with much truth—why should we go to primaries ?   We can have no influence there unless we surrender

our opinions and independence to those who control these organizations; why should we vote? We have only a choice between two
candidates, both unworthy. When this subject was discussed in the
British Parliament some years ago, Lord Cairns said: "With regard
to the constituency itself—and this is one of the most important views
of the case—I believe you would gain the greatest possible satisfaction;
there is nothing so irksome to those who form the minority of one of
those large constituencies as finding that from mere force of numbers
they are virtually excluded from the exercise of any political power; that
it is vain for them to attempt to take any part in public affairs; that
the elections must go in one direction, and that they have no political
power whatever. On the one hand the result is great dissatisfaction,
and on the other it is disinclination on the part of those who form the
minority to take any part in affairs in which it is important they should
take a prominent and conspicuous part."

In the same debate Mr. Buxton said: "They (the minority) feel it
totally hopeless to attempt to carry a candidate, and they resign themselves with more or less bitterness to political death. They feel that they
are altogether excluded from any influence whatever over the destinies
of their country: not merely that they cannot hope to rule, but that
they cannot even be represented in the council of the nation. They
accordingly sink into hopeless apathy, while the majority having everything their own way, not enjoying the advantage of being opposed and
forced to struggle and strive, would themselves also be likely to grow at
once apathetic and arrogant. He was not devising this state of things out
of his own imagination; they knew that exactly this had happened in
many instances both across the water and in certain constituencies at
home when one party * * * had held irresistible sway.

"But now suppose * * * the arrangement proposed (propor-.
tional representation) were adopted; immediately every elector in
the constituency would be stirred into life. Those who belonged to
the minority instead of giving up the whole affair as a bad job, shrug-
ging their shoulders, and feeling that although they were Englishmen
they were as destitute of political influence as if they were so many
Indians, would immediately organize themselves as a party to form a
committee to look out for a candidate and combine to carry him.

* * *   Political deadness would be exchanged for political anima-
tion.''

It was said in the Address to the Public of the American Proportional
Representation League : '' When every citizen votes with the full assur-
ance that each individual vote bears directly upon the final result, the
men who have withdrawn in despair from politics as something with
which an honest man can have nothing to do, will return to their duty.''

In his article already quoted from Mr. Leonard Courtney said, that
with minority representation '' you will have a real and not an artificial democracy.   According to the idea of this system any adequate
number could join together, select their man, and send him in.   It
follows that if there arose a political thinker in the country, men would
come together throughout the country and return him.   Men would
gather round him and send him in, and you would thus have introduced into the House of Commons elements of life, strengthening and
vivifying the whole ; instead of making mediocrity a condition without which nobody could enter, you would have life and energy secured
in the return of able men ; and of course if you got candidates thus
independent you would change the House of Commons, and you would
operate upon the people outside.''

As some one else has said : '' While it is constantly for the interest
of cliques and minorities to put knaves and simpletons into office, it
never can be to the interest of the majority to be represented by them.''
The majority of our fellow citizens wish to be represented by the ablest
and best men that the community can furnish ; and Mr. Mill has said :
'' The multitude have often a fine instinct for distinguishing an able man
when he has the means of displaying his ability in a fair field.''   Give
them freedom of selection and the people of the country, it is believed,
may be trusted to select able and also honest men.

CHAPTER XI.

It may be thought that a system of free voting like that which has been described may diminish the influence of party organization in political affairs. Undoubtedly it would give greater independence to individual voters, but this would make it none the less possible to combine for party purposes, if such combination were desirable. Regarding this Mr. Buckalew will again be quoted : "So long," he said, "as free play is permitted to the human mind in political affairs, there will be parties, and government must be organized and administered with reference to them, and that all attempts based upon the assumption that it is possible to conduct public affairs without parties, are idle and vain ; in fine, that all attempts based on that idea must result in complete and disastrous failure. No such object has been proposed by persons in this country, or beyond the ocean, who have supported this plan of the free vote or cumulative voting. All they propose is to put into the hands of political parties an instrument by which they can act justly at elections, by which they can obtain for themselves a fair share of power by their own votes and by which it will be impossible for them to take from their fellow-citizens any portion of political power which belongs to *them*."

Discussing this same branch of the subject an' English writer * in the *Westminster Review* for January, 1884, says :

"A system of preferential voting takes from party organization none of its legitimate influence and power, but it gives any section of the party dissatisfied with the choice of their local association an appeal from its decision. Without endangering the seat they may, if they can, start a more satisfactory candidate, and can take the opinion of the constituency upon the merits of the rivals, not by any fallacious party vote, taken beforehand, but by a test-ballot forming part of the actual process of election. Under these circumstances the association (caucus) will no longer enjoy the dangerous privilege of irresponsible

---

* J. Parker Smith.

and absolute authority, but will be in the position of a constitutional ministry liable to have their decisions reversed and discredited unless they can carry along with them the majority of their party."

While free voting is adapted to party organization it also facilitates, as Mr. Buckalew says, "the bolting of nominations by an aggrieved interest, for such interest, if of respectable size, can represent, by its own votes, without disturbing or changing the whole result of an election. * * *

"Bolting is deprived to a great extent of its mischievous character, bolters being only able to represent themselves by their own votes when their number is adequate, without being able to turn an election upside down or prevent a just division of the offices between parties."

"Proportional representation," Prof. John R. Commons * says, "would permit independent movements within the party without risking the defeat of the entire ticket, simply by allowing the nomination of a new ticket composed partly of independents and partly of the regular ticket."

One of the great evils of democratic government, which is especially noticeable in great cities, is the facility with which the most ignorant and venal voters can be combined and controlled—as Mr. Sterne says —"by men with penetration enough to discover the weaknesses, the follies, and the vices of their neighbors, and who are both skillful and unscrupulous enough to make them subservient to their own ends." It may be added that *venality* is often the only weakness, folly and vice which need be discovered in order to make such voters subservient to the purposes of corrupt politicians.   The influence of such bodies of voters, thus controlled, given to either of the dominant parties, will often decide which one of them will be in a majority, in districts in which a single representative is elected.   Unfortunately the organization of the intelligent and the worthier electors is not so effective in controlling elections, because, owing to the fact that they hold some definite political principles, or possibly prejudices, they, for that reason, give their adherence or votes to one party or the other, while

---

* Proportional Representation a Remedy for Gerrymandering, a paper submitted to the American Academy of Political and Social Science.

those who determine on which side the majority shall be are not encumbered by any such scruples, but vote, "for revenue only." The method of the practical politicians is a very simple one and one which they have not been slow in comprehending. It is briefly this—first announce in the "platforms" of each of the two dominant parties some general principles and measures which will secure the adherence of nearly equal portions of the honest voters to each. This will leave a remnant of say one-fifth or some other fraction of all the voters. All that is needed then to carry the election, is to cajole or to bribe *a majority* of this unrighteous remnant. The professional politicians are not usually slow to work the corrupt remnant, in their vernacular, "for all it is worth." The political influence of the intelligent, upright and worthy portion of the community is therefore, generally, "in the inverse ratio of their mental and moral capacity and value. Unless this evil is encountered by giving to intellect and integrity a greater freedom and effectiveness of action—not freedom to bribe and cajole ; but freedom for pure and honorable effort—and therewith, higher and better inducements to act, will surely leave them in this country as elsewhere in like circumstances, degraded and powerless." *

The reform of our elective machinery which is advocated would make combinations of the better elements in society easier and more effective in political affairs than they can possibly be now. It is true that the corrupt portion of the voters would have equal facilities for combining but they would no longer be able to control political affairs, and their sole object and that of their leaders is to *control* the power, patronage and "boodle." Take away their power to do this and the motive for their being "in politics" is gone. As the Hon. Charles Francis Adams said in a recent article in the *Proportional Representation Review :*

"Consider what an enormous influence this would give to the intelligent individual voter! How it would bother the municipal 'boss !' Voters are now divided up and segregated by artificial lines ; they are in this way so placed that they can be manipulated by astute political managers to the utmost possible extent. Their efforts at a better state of things can be thwarted. Under the system pro-

---

* Thomas Hare in *Macmillan's Magazine*, February, 1862.

posed they would be free from all restraints and put in position where the individual could make himself felt, provided he desired so to do. He could not be tied hand and foot.

"Take the city of New York. We all know the character of those composing the legislative department of the city. It is notorious—it could not be worse than it is. Suppose that instead of the present board of aldermen and its common council the city of New York were to elect one legislative body in such a way that every proportionate part of the voters should have one representative. Suppose every vote to bear directly upon the final result, with all useless majorities and wasted minorities given their proper effect. If the council consisted of 21 members any body of citizens numbering one 21st part of the whole number of voters could and would have one representative. Would not the inevitable result be the nomination as candidates by citizen organizations of at least a certain number of men, who, if elected would give weight and character to that body? Would not the result naturally be that men of the class now composing the legislative department of New York city either would not be brought forward as candidates at all, or if brought forward before the constituency as a whole, and no longer in wards, would be left in the election at the foot of the poll? Every reform organization hoping to represent one twenty-first part of the total vote thrown would be under the highest possible inducement to put forward as its candidate the man of the strongest character, and the man most widely and favorably known. The objection to bringing forward men who were only locally known would be equally great. The object of each organization would necessarily be to nominate candidates who would draw to themselves the greatest number of votes in the constituency at large. The political prison lines, now known as ward lines, would be thrown down."

CHAPTER XII.

But it may be said as Disraeli did say that, "cumulative voting, and other schemes having for their object to represent minorities, that they were admirable schemes for bringing crotchety men into the House," or as John Bright said, they would "put in the nominees of little cliques," or to quote Gladstone's words, "we do not want to have represented immature particular shades of opinion." Now what is a "crotchet"? Nearly all legislative innovations are, at first, regarded as being "crotchets"—or, as the dictionary expresses it, "perverse fancies." If as De Quincey said, "these cannot be explained to any rational man," then of course it is not desirable that they should have representation. The abolition of slavery, the establishing of free trade and civil service reform, and even honesty in the public service, all were, or are, regarded as *crotchets*. If opinions are held by any *considerable* body of men even if they are crotchets it is altogether better that they should have a *fair* hearing. If they cannot be "explained to rational people," the hearing will do little harm. Mr. Bright's remark is perhaps true that "*little*" cliques should not be heard in the halls of legislature, but the force of his remark is in the word "*little*." Ought *big* "cliques" to be heard, that is, if any considerable body of intelligent voters hold any opinions relating to the conduct of public affairs, ought they to be heard? It may be true, as Gladstone said, that "*immature particular* shades of opinion" ought not to be represented, but if the shades of opinion are *mature* and *generally* held by a sufficient number of people, so as to form *important political interests* in the country then they should have representation and be heard, even though those who hold such opinions are not in a majority. It is true that the time of legislative bodies and the patience of legislators ought not to be consumed and wasted by "cranks" and "wind-bags," but, as a writer in the *North American Review* in 1862*, said: "If the

---

* P. 240.

legislative assembly be in its prime intent and use a parliament, a talking body, *every numerous and respectable party* among the people has an undoubted right to its share in the *talk;* every significant phasis of opinion has a right to be presented and advocated ; or, to state the case still more strongly, the nation has a right to such practical wisdom as can be elicited only by the free comparison and discussion of opposing and divergent theories and measures ; and the legislators who represent a bare majority have no right to close their ears and minds to the most ample and forceful presentation of the views and arguments of the minority.''

Mr. Gladstone in his discussion of this question laid down that '' the principle of parliamentary representation is that we should recognize each constituency as being in itself an integer, and what we want in the House is the prevailing sense of the community.'' Now is it more philosophical and just to regard bare majorities in restricted geographical districts as political '' integers '' or considerable bodies of qualified voters holding common opinions, having like interests, and whose '' wills are in harmony with respect to the reciprocal rights of men and social relations,'' but who are scattered over wider areas than the present constituencies are ? Just representation it would seem should be based on the theory that bodies of people whose interests and opinions are harmonious are the true political integers which ought to be heard.

The strong argument though which is advanced by the opponents of minority representation is that '' it is desirable that the party which has a majority in the country should have a good working majority, considering the power of obstruction even a small minority can exert. Is it not therefore desirable that the majority in Parliament should be greater than that in the country ? '' It has been said that it is a mistake to assume that the main object of law is to administer justice— that—it is asserted—is only an incident to its operation—but its main purpose is to end dispute and contention. So it may be said of legislative bodies that it is not of the utmost importance that their acts should be the wisest possible, but they should be *decisive* so as to maintain '' law.'' The argument of the opponents of minority representation is that it will weaken the *decisiveness* of governments, by reducing majorities. But this occurs under the present system where opinions in legislative bodies are nearly evenly balanced, as they often are, and, if public opinion is very equally divided is it not better, in every way, that both sides should at least be fully heard? When elections are decided by bare majorities, it often happens that there are sudden changes and one party is turned out and another put in. A vacillating government, or one which changes suddenly from one side to the other of important questions, is worse than one with a small majority. When majorities are very large parties for that reason are liable to split into factions and become disorganized. When public opinion is emphatic the government may also be so, but when there is a nearly equal division of opinion government should be cautious and conservative.

Considerable complaint comes from Illinois of the narrowness of the majority in the House of Representatives, in that state, owing to the representation of both parties through cumulative voting.

The following are some of the opinions received in reply to the circular of inquiry :

" The majority ought to rule and it does not always rule under the cumulative system." Rep. *Springfield.*

" It gives in Illinois Republican representatives in Democratic districts and Democratic representatives in Republican districts. Thus it weakens the dominant party and so far as I can see helps none but it gives the minority a representation everywhere." Rep. *Sandwich.*

" In some instances the system has so equally divided the members of our legislature politically as to prevent action. The cumulative system would give minorities in Congress and in the boards sufficient strength as to prevent action." Dem. *Anna.*

" Some of the disadvantages are, the legislature is too close—as instance U. S. senatorships that have been obtained in this state by questionable means—that is never a majority of more than a dozen, and it is very often two or three ; that you will concede is too close, it is not a good working majority." Rep. *Austin.*

" The worst result of the system is that it gives the minority undue strength and advantage. In Illinois under this system the minority may be said to control legislation, for the legislature is usually so evenly balanced that the majority party, which is held responsible for the acts of the session, finds its hands tied and can do little without the consent of the minority.   It has happened also that the minority party has gained control of the lower house, though the majority against them in the state was large.   Great and desirable reforms in legislation have been hindered and defeated because of this.   The two parties being so evenly balanced that each could throw the blame of failure on the other. In our system of government the majority must be held responsible for legislation, and a system that gives the minority almost equal strength and puts every weapon of obstruction and hindrance in its hands is not a good system.''   Rep. *Pontiac.*

The mathematics of this objection does not, however, seem to be quite satisfactory or conclusive, for the reason that what a party would gain in one section it would be likely to lose in another.   Thus the northern part of Illinois is predominantly Republican and the southern half* Democratic, consequently the influence of the one section would counteract that of the other.   In the State of New York the Republicans would gain largely in the city of New York, by free voting, but would lose in the rural districts.   In Illinois the state senators are elected by a majority of the voters in single districts, while the members of the House are elected on the cumulative plan.   In 1892 there were 22 Republican and 29 Democratic senators elected.   The House consisted of 75 Republicans and 78 Democrats.   It is true the majority of the Democrats in the senate was larger than in the House, but the difference is not greater than might be accounted for by accidental circumstances or as the result, possibly, of the gerrymander.

When this subject was under discussion ten or more years ago, in England, Mr. Bright ''claimed to have demolished John Stuart Mill and his views on proportional representation, to the effect that if proportional representation had been the practice in the United States at the time of the war of secession that it would have been impossible to have prosecuted it or abolished slavery.

'' The answer to Mr. Bright is that if proportional representation had been the principle on which their elections had been conducted,

---

*The extreme southern counties are also Republican.

slavery would have been abolished, and the war would never have taken place." *

Of this Prof. Ware in his article in the *American Law Review* said :

" Could the principle of proportional representation have been recognized in the composition of the House of Representatives twenty years ago, it would have introduced into Congress a large number of northern Democrats and southern Whigs, occupying a middle ground and holding the balance of power—men out of favor at home, but strong enough both in numbers and position to check the violence that led at last to the civil war."

This statement was emphatically accepted and endorsed by the senate committee in their report on representative reform, to which reference has already been made. According to that report, the declared opinion of the picked and chosen members of the United States Senate is :

" The absence of the cumulative vote in the states of the south, when rebellion was plotted, and when open steps were taken to break the Union, was unfortunate, for it would have held the union men of those states together, and given them voice in the electoral colleges and in Congress.

" But they were fearfully overborne by the plurality rule of elections, and were swept forward by the course of events into impotency or open hostility to our cause. By that rule they were shut out of the electoral colleges. Dispersed, unorganized, unrepresented, without due voice ànd power, they could interpose no effectual resistance to secession and to civil war ; their leaders were struck down at unjust elections, and could not speak or act for them in their own states or at the capital of the nation.

" By facts well known to us we are assured that the leaders of the revolt with much difficulty carried their states with them. Even in Georgia, the empire state of the south, the scale was almost balanced for a time, and in most of these states it required all the machinery and influence of a vicious electoral system to organize the war against us, and hold those communities compactly as our foes."

*Albert Grey, in *Nineteenth Century* of December, 1884.

The strong argument in reply to the objection that a government in which all bodies of opinions and interests are represented will be less decisive than one in which local majorities control is that: "there will be less fluctuation under a system of proportional representation, because the people who fluctuate will affect only their own quotas, instead of affecting the representation of those who are staunch by turning the majorities in a large number of districts. Now a steady pressure is not less potent for progressive legislation, and is more likely to be wisely applied than an occasional rush. The majorities obtained by large turn-overs are in truth too insecure in themselves to afford steady support to a minister."*

Another argument that is often urged against minority representation is that the plan destroys the local character of the representation. Of this argument Mr. Mill observed: "Every constituency, it is said, is a group, having certain interests and feelings in common, and if you disperse these groups by allowing the electors to group themselves in other combinations, those interests and feelings will be deprived of their representation. Now I fully admit that the interests and feelings of localities ought to be represented, and I add that they always will be represented, because those interests and feelings exist in the minds of the electors; and as the plan I propose has no effect but to give the freest and fullest play to the individual electors over preferences, his local preferences are certain to exercise their proper amount of influence. I do not know what better guardian of a feeling can be wanted than the man who feels it, or how it is possible for a man to have a vote, and not carry his interests and feelings, local as well as general, with him to the polling booth. Indeed, it may be set down as certain that the majority of voters in every locality will generally prefer to be represented by one of themselves, who is connected with the place by some special tie. It is chiefly those who know themselves to be locally in a minority, and unable to elect a local representative of their opinions, who would avail themselves of the liberty of voting on the new principle. As far as the majority were concerned, the only effect would be that their local leaders would have a greatly increased motive to find out and bring forward the best local candidate

* *Nineteenth Century*, February, 1885.

that could be had, because the electors, having the power of transferring their votes elsewhere, would demand a candidate whom they
would feel it a credit to vote for. The average quality of the local
representative would consequently be improved, but local interests and
feelings would still be represented, as they cannot possibly fail to be,
as long as every elector resides in a locality."

This is in substance saying that if electors regard their local interests as of more importance than general interests they can and probably will vote for some one who will represent their local interests
most satisfactorily. If on the other hand they are most concerned in
some measures relating to the general public weal, then they would
select and vote for the candidate or candidates who would most satisfactorily represent these interests. In other words they would be FREE
to vote for the promotion of either local or general interests as they
choose or possibly for both. The question then arises whether it is
desirable that electors should be at liberty to give their political influence for the advancement of those interests which they regard as being
the most important be they local or general. Probably few voters will
hesitate about deciding in favor of the greatest freedom in the exercise
of the right of suffrage.

Besides this reason, as Mr. Horton has said, " the argument in favor
of the single district that it gives district local interests a hearing, is
to-day in part neutralized by the rapidity of travel and the facilities of
communication." As another writer has said : " the end and object
of reform, whatever it may be, is best attained by the representation of
electors and not of *localities*." Mr. Courtney * stated this argument
very well in saying that " there would be no more loss of local feeling than the people living in localities wish to lose. If people are so
animated with a local feeling that they must vote for one man in their
own neighborhood, they would have perfect liberty so to do. You
give them power to join with those who are allied with them in feeling and thought, instead of with those who live next door ; but you
don't force them to go afield, and whenever local wants demanded
local representation they would be sure to secure it."

Furthermore, where is the justice or the wisdom of refusing to

---

* *Nineteenth Century* for July, 1879.

authorize a man to make laws for us because he lives on the other side of some arbitrary line which separates one district from another.   As Mr. Quincy* has said : " Is there any person outside of politics, and outside a mad-house, who desires a law to forbid him from employing a worthy man, whether as blacksmith, doctor, lawyer or legislator because he lives in an adjoining town, or perhaps across the street in the next ward ? "

Sometimes the principle of local representation is reduced to an absurdity.   Thus in the lower wards of New York city there is property the value of which is probably greater than that in any equal area in the world and amounts to many millions ; and yet, in those wards, almost, if not quite, the only persons who vote for representatives, from these districts, in Congress, the state legislature and the common council of the city, *are the janitors of the buildings*, as they are the only residents in these districts.

---

* " The Protection of Majorities," by Josiah Phillips Quincy, 1879.

CHAPTER XIII.

It may, not unfairly, be asked what would be gained, practically, if the system of free voting which has been described were adopted in the city and State of New York, or in other cities and states, and we were to elect say seven representatives to our state and municipal legislative bodies from each district enlarged with that object in view?

It may be replied in the first place, it would make it possible for any body of voters exceeding an eighth of all in the district to elect a candidate by uniting and casting all their votes for him. That this could be done can be shown by an assumed example : Supposing that there are 30,632 voters in a district, in which seven representatives are to be elected, then one-eighth of the voters plus 1 would be equal to 3830. It will be supposed that our hypothetical district is located in one of the strong Democratic sections of New York city and that 22,-972 voters are Democrats and 7660 are Republicans. The Democrats let it be assumed, are confident, as they have been in the past, that they can carry everything before them and therefore they nominate a full ticket of seven candidates for aldermen. *A, B, C, D, E, F* and *G,* let us say, and all the voters being loyal to the ticket vote it "straight." The Republicans being in a very decided minority nominate only three candidates, *H, I* and *J,* and they all vote their regular ticket. The results of the election would then be as shown in the third column of the table on next page.

It will be supposed further that when the voting is completed and all the votes in the districts have been counted, that the Burnitz method, for the final computation is employed, that is, *the total number of first choice votes for each candidate to be divided by 1, the total number of second choice votes by 2, the third choice by 3, and so on.* If this is done and if the seven candidates who receive the highest quotients are elected it will be seen that the 7660 Republicans in this district have elected two of their men. This they can do under the

Burnitz system of free voting in spite of any combination which the Democrats can make against them.

DEMOCRATIC VOTE.			REPUBLICAN VOTE.		
1	2	3	1	2	3
Candidate.	Votes.	Quotients	Candidate.	Votes.	Quotients
1st A	22,972	22,972	1st H	7,660˙	7,660
2d B	22,972	11,486	2d. I	7,660	3,830
3d C	22,972	7,657⅓	3d J	7,660	~~2,553⅓~~
4th D	22,972	5,743			
5th E	22,972	4,594⅖			
6th F	22,972	~~3,828⅔~~			
7th G	22,972	~~3,281⅔~~			

The principle on which this result is based may be expressed mathematically if we suppose N equals the total number of votes, then

$$\tfrac{1}{8}\, N + 1 > \frac{\tfrac{7}{8}\, N - 1}{7} = \tfrac{1}{8}\, N - \tfrac{1}{7}$$

In other words, one-eighth of *all* the votes + 1 vote (or any other number) is greater than one-seventh of the remainder of all the votes. Consequently if one candidate gets *more* than one-eighth of the votes there will not be enough left to give each of seven candidates more than that number.

Another illustration of the working of the system may be given. Supposing that the two dominant parties should, as they often do now, nominate unfit candidates, and the intelligent and respectable independent voters in the district revolt and conclude to make nominations and run candidates of their own.   Not being sure of their strength, but hoping to be able to elect more than one candidate, they conclude to put two in the field.   It will be supposed that the Democrats run seven candidates, *A, B, C, D, E, F* and *G* and the Republicans five, *H, I, J, K* and *L* and the Independents two, *O* and *P*, and that the vote is as follows :   Democrats, 19,221 ; Republicans, 17,917 ; Independents, 7430.   The result under the Burnitz system of free voting would be as shown in the following table :

DEMOCRATIC.			REPUBLICAN.			INDEPENDENT.		
1 Cand.	2 Votes.	3 Quotients	1 Cand.	2 Votes.	3 Quotients	1 Cand.	2 Votes.	3 Quotients
1st A	19,221	19,221	1st H	17,917	17,917	1st O	7,430	7,430
2d B	19,221	9,610½	2d I	17,917	8,958½	2d P	7,430	~~3,715~~
3d C	19,221	6,407	3d J	17,917	5,972⅓			
4th D	19,221	~~4,805¼~~	4th K	17,917	~~4,479¼~~			
5th E	19,221	~~3,844~~	5th L	17,917	~~3,583⅖~~			
6th F	19,221	~~3,203½~~						
7th G	19,221	~~2,603~~						

That is, the Democratic and Republican parties would both elect three candidates and the Independents one.   It is true that in this ·case the Democrats have more votes than the Republicans, they both elect the same number of candidates.   The Republicans and Independents together get four representatives but as their aggregate numbers exceed the Democrats this result is fair.   Evidently there is more justice in such a result than ordinarily follows where single representatives are elected from each district.   It has already been stated that in 1892, although the Republicans had nearly 100,000 voters in the city of New York they did not elect a single alderman, assemblyman or state senator.

But the operation of such a system would have other very important consequences.   It would as has been shown enable any body of voters exceeding one-eighth to elect their candidate.   The effect. of this would be that they would be freed from the tyranny of the caucus and '' machine politics,'' because by nominating their own candidate and concentrating their votes on him any fractional part of the voters in a district, exceeding an eighth, could elect one or more representatives in spite of the political managers.   What is perhaps of equal importance, they would be able to reëlect him and keep him in office so long as he represented them satisfactorily. This would give to a representative much more independence than he can have if his election is dependent upon a fickle majority of all the voters in a smaller district. Under the system which is here advocated he would owe his election to the votes of a comparatively small and select constituency having interests, opinions and political principles which he has been chosen—and which he is presumably fitted—to represent, and, so long as he does this to the satisfaction of those who elected him, they can, if they choose, continue him in office. In the performance of his duties he would have only the demands of his own individual constituents to satisfy, and would not be obliged to make his opinions and conduct concur with the views, the prejudices, the ignorance and perhaps the vices of some of those who help to form a popular majority.

The system of free voting which is advocated herein, would give the most intelligent and best educated classes in the community the power to choose and elect men of distinguished ability as their representatives, a privilege which under the existing condition of things they can rarely do now. In discussing this side of the subject Mr. Mill said :

" The natural tendency of representative government, as of modern civilization, is towards collective mediocrity ; and this tendency is increased by all reductions and extensions of the franchise, their effect being to place the principal power in the hands of classes more and more below the highest level of instruction in the community. But, though the superior intellects and characters will necessary be outnumbered, it makes a great difference whether they are heard. In the false democracy which, instead of giving representation to all, gives it only to the local majorities, the voice of the instructed minority may have no organs at all in the representative body."

Although the following remarks by Mr. Mill referred to the Hare system of electing representatives, the arguments are equally cogent in support of the system of free voting advocated here.

" The minority of instructed minds," he says, " scattered through the local constituencies would unite to return a number proportioned to their own numbers of the ablest men the country contains. They would be under the strongest inducement to choose such men, since in no other mode could they make their small numerical strength tell for anything considerable. The representatives of the majority, besides that they would themselves be improved in quality by the operation of the system, would no longer have the whole field to themselves. They would indeed outnumber the others, as much as the one class of electors outnumbers the other in the country ; they could always outvote them, but they would speak and vote in their presence, and subject to their criticism. When any difference arose they would have to meet the arguments of the instructed few by reasons, at least apparently, as cogent ; and since they could not, as those do who are speaking to persons already unanimous, simply assume that they are in the right, it would occasionally happen to them to become convinced that they were in the wrong. As they would in general be well-meaning (for this much may reasonably be expected from a fairly-chosen national representative), their own minds would be insensibly raised by the influence of the minds with which they were in contact, or even in conflict. The champions of unpopular doctrines would not put forth their arguments merely in books and periodicals, read only by their own side ; the opposing ranks would meet face to face and hand to hand, and there would be a fair comparison of their intellectual strength in the presence of the country. It would then be found out whether the opinion which prevailed by counting votes would also prevail if the votes were weighed as well as counted. *The multitude have often a true instinct for distinguishing an able man when he has the means of displaying his ability in a fair field before them.* *. * * If the presence in the representative assembly can be insured of even a few of the first minds in the country, though the remainder consist only of average minds, the influence of these leading spirits is sure to make itself insensibly felt in the general deliberations, even though they be known to be, in many respects, opposed to the tone of popular opinion and feeling. * * *

" The only quarter in which to look for a supplement, or completing corrective to the instincts of a democratic majority, is the instructed minority ; but, in the ordinary mode of constituting democracy, this minority has no organ. * * * The representatives who would be returned by the aggregate of minorities would afford that organ in its greatest perfection. A separate organization of the instructed classes, even if practicable, would be invidious, and could only escape from being offensive by being totally without influence. But if the *élite* of these classes formed part of the parliament, by the same title as any other of its members, by representing the same number of citizens, the same numerical fraction of the national will—their presence would give umbrage to nobody, while they would be in the position of highest vantage, both for making their opinions and counsels heard on all important subjects, and for taking an active part in public business. Their abilities would probably draw to them more than their numerical share of the actual administration of government. * * * The instructed minority would, in the actual voting, count only for their numbers, but as a moral power they would count for much more, in virtue of their knowledge, and of the influence it would give them over the rest. An arrangement better adapted to keep popular opinion within reason and justice, and to guard it from the various deteriorating influences which assail the weak side of democracy, could scarcely by human ingenuity be devised. A democratic people would in this way be provided with what in any other way it would almost certainly miss—leaders of a higher grade of intellect and character than itself. Modern democracy would have its occasional Pericles, and its habitual group of superior and guiding minds.''

As Dr. Holmes says, not only are there two sides to every question, but most subjects appear to be at least hexagonal. This one seems to be of that kind, and Mr. Quincy in looking at another side of this ideal polyhedron says :

" While it is a matter of serious concern that so many men of high intelligence and sturdy character are virtually disfranchised by the caucus system, it is no less unfortunate that the great body of laboring men are nearly as powerless in the hands of the managers. Our social organization, which has experienced so great changes in the past, is destined to profound modifications in the future. Whether these shall come about violently or gradually, whether we shall rise to a nobler civilization, or pass into a period of chaos, depends upon the adequate representation of the working classes. Plato has significantly told us that each Grecian state enclosed two states—one composed of the rich, the other of the poor. Our American states are coming to be divided in the same way; and, under the management of caucus politicians, the dividing line will be constantly deepening. Manual labor has no adequate representation in our government. The money powers and knavish combinations which hold sway in the caucus have too often offered the workingman only a choice between two evils.''

The system of election which is advocated here, would give to any body of workingmen, exceeding an eighth of the voters in a district, the power to elect a representative of their own, and they could do this independently of any caucus or alliances with party managers by which their own real interests would be bargained for and bought and sold by cunning, adroit and unscrupulous party managers. Under this system laboring men would have the same independence that it would give to those who have been favored with all the advantages which are derived from education, knowledge and superior opportunities. Not that the interests of these two classes are in any sense antagonistic, for as Mr. Quincy well says : ''in the last analysis we shall always find that the real and permanent interest of any class is identical with the real and permanent interest of all classes. * * * Men of independent thought, thorough instruction, and high morality, are the natural allies of the humble and the wronged ; but such men are as worthless to the political managers as they are precious to the people.''

It is probable too, that nothing would do so much to enlighten working men with reference to their political rights, duties and relations as to be represented by members of their own selection, elected by their own votes and sent to our legislative bodies to speak for the people who sent them there. Such representatives would be obliged, as Mr. Mill says, ''to meet the opposing ranks face to face and hand to hand, and there would be a fair comparison of their intellectual strength in the presence of the country,'' and the representatives of the laboring men ''would have to meet the arguments of the instructed few by reasons, at least apparently, as cogent,'' and as the same author significantly says, '' it would occasionally happen to them to become convinced that they were in the wrong." The converse of this, in all probability, would sometimes occur, that is the "instructed few" would be convinced by the representatives of the workingmen of the ·justice and righteousness of the claims and interests of "labor." In this view, what could be more wholesome for the whole body politic, in the present condition of discontent among workingmen and the antagonism that so often exists between them and their employers, than to have the former, as well as the latter, fairly represented in our legislative bodies. The workingmen with the limited educational advantages which most of them have had, and oftener still, with more limited pecuniary resources, their lack of knowledge and experience in the management of political affairs, their ignorance of the principles in accordance with which wise legislation must be framed, are often moulded by the corrupt politicians to serve their uses, as clay is shaped by the potter, or are kneaded like dough in the hands of the baker, only to have their just interests neglected later and to be flattered and cajoled when their votes are again needed. Under the present system of electing representatives the only way that workingmen can secure representation is by coöperation with the political managers. While the latter are bargaining for the votes of the men, they are also trading with those whom the men regard as their antagonists, and thus the true interests of both parties are "sold out" before the member to be elected gets into office or power. Free voting would make it possible for workingmen to choose, nominate and elect their own candidates independently of the politicians and without their agency or coöperation. It would give to the working classes real *freedom* and independence in the election of their representatives. The system therefore appeals with great force to laborers, workingmen and mechanics of all classes for their support. It will place in their hands an instrumentality, which will give them the power to be represented by members of their own selection, in all legislative bodies, who may be true and faithful advocates of their real interests, and be untrammeled by bargains with those whom the men regard as their oppressors.

But the great and incontestible argument in favor of free voting is its inherent justice not to *one* class alone, but to all classes, as it will enable any considerable body of voters in any district to secure representation. The principle upon which it is based is that the opinions of the entire people, and not those of a mere majority alone, should be represented in our legislative bodies, and that in them minorities as · well as majorities, advocates and opponents, petitions, remonstrances, and protests of all sorts and what may be regarded as heresies as well, may all be represented and are entitled to a hearing.

What Professor Ware said in his article in the *American Law Review* for Jan., 1872, of other similar schemes of electoral reform, is equally true of the one which is advocated here. " In the first place " he says, " the representative body itself would promise to be not only more justly but more efficiently made up. Not only would the proper political organizations be more fully represented, and that under conditions likely to bring out their best men, but other interests which at present have no hearing, or at least are heard of only through the politicians, could, if they saw fit, send their own men, and their best men, to speak for them. There could hardly fail to result a deliberative body far beyond what we are in the habit of seeing, in point of ability and character, embracing a much greater range of knowledge and experience, and embodying a much greater variety of opinion and conviction. Such a body, truly representative, and containing within itself the accredited agents of all parties and interests, need not look to the newspapers or to the lobby for facts or for arguments. It would be competent to do its appointed work of investigation and discussion, and gain in self-respect and in public estimation accordingly. The more this was felt to be the case, the more it would come to ' be perceived that real head work was being done, the more careful would all parties and interests become to be represented by their best men. It is true that the scheme of proportional representation would permit the extremists to send extreme men. But it would also permit moderate men to be represented by men of their own kind,—a kind which the majority rule is sure in times of excitement, when they are most needed, to send to the wall."

Or, as another writer* has said, by the representation of minorities " you will have a real and not an artificial democracy. According to

* Leonard Courtney in the *Nineteenth Century* for July, 1879.

the idea of this system any adequate number could join together, select their man and send him in. It follows that if there arose a political thinker in the country, men would come together throughout the country and return him. Men would gather round him and send him in, and you would thus have introduced into the House of Commons elements of life, strengthening and vivifying the whole ; instead of making mediocrity a condition without which nobody could enter, you would have life and energy secured in the return of able men, and of course if you got candidates thus independent you would change the House of Commons, and you would operate upon the people outside."

This is equally as true and as applicable to our own national, state and municipal bodies as it is to the British Parliament.

The same writer says further : " One great result that would arise from the reform would be disintegration of party. Parties would not cling together so closely as they do now. * * * You would more freely detach men, one by one, from any majority. At present scarcely any member of a party ever dares desert it ; but if a man had not to depend for his seat on mere party cohesion within a limited area—if he knew that his independence would bring support from a wider range—you would have more freedom of thought, and there would be more room for conversion than you now have. Not that men are not converted now. Many are converted in their minds, but they do not change their votes."

But to those of us who for years have been tyrannized over by ignorant, corrupt and debased political bosses ; who have been humiliated beyond expression by their overbearing insolence ; who have been overwhelmed with shame by the demoralization and putrescence of our municipal, state and sometimes the national governments ; and who are full of indignation and ready for lawful rebellion to release ourselves from the iniquitous reign under which we are living—the contemplation of a condition of things under which the reputable and decent portions of the community could bid defiance to our despised oppressors, fills us with hope and should inspire all who yearn for freedom to exertion and effort to throw off the yoke which now oppresses us. The adoption of a system of Free Voting would overthrow the bosses, would undermine their power, spread consternation in their ranks and make us all free. Or as the editor* of Mr. Buckalew's book on Proportional Representation, has said in his preface :

"'The reform when accepted generally, will purify elections, establish justice in representation, elevate the tone of public life and give additional credit and lustre to that system of government by the people which is our proudest boast, and our best legacy for those who come after us."

To the pessimists who despair of ever effecting so desirable a reform, the language of Mr. Hare, the apostle of minority representation, may be quoted :

"'The quiet admission," he said, " that we are all of us so ready to make, that, because things have long been wrong, it is impossible they should ever be right, is one of the most fatal sources of misery and crime from which the world suffers. Whenever you hear a man dissuading you from attempting to do well, on the ground that perfection is 'utopian,' beware of that man. Cut the word out of your dictionary altogether. There is no need for it. Things are either possible or impossible ; you can easily determine which, in any given state of human science. If the thing is impossible, you need not trouble yourselves about it ; if possible, try for it. It is very utopian to hope for the entire doing away of drunkenness and misery out of the Cannongate ; but the utopianism is not our business—the *work* is."

---

* John G. Freeze.

THE END.

APPENDIX A.

Under the cumulative system, which has little or no capacity for automatic adaptation, as one of our correspondents from Illinois pointed out, and as the reports of the working of that system in the election of members of English school boards indicate, "a voter cannot tell when he is casting more votes than a favorite candidate needs." If a larger number of candidates are elected by that system from each district than are now elected in Illinois, then this difficulty will be increased in a considerably greater ratio than the increase of the numbers to be elected. If a greater number are not elected in each district than are now returned in Illinois, then the freedom of voters is curtailed in about an inverse proportion to the number elected.

As a remedy for these evils what is known as the quota system has been proposed. A number of such plans have been devised which differ from each other in their details, but may generally be described as follows: The total number of votes cast at an election in a general district is divided by the number of representatives to be elected. The quotient forms the electoral basis, or "quota," that is to say, every candidate obtaining this "quota" of votes shall be elected.* No more than the quota strictly necessary for his election is counted in favor of any candidate. The surplusage of votes given to any elected candidate is to be distributed in favor of other candidates.

The great difficulty about most, if not all, of the plans of this kind which have been proposed, is first, as John Bright perhaps jeeringly said, very few people can understand them. The next difficulty is in deciding which of the votes obtained by each candidate shall count for his own election, and which of them shall be released in favor of other candidates. One of the writers† in describing the Hare system

* This is the "quota" adopted by some of the advocates of this plan. It has been shown though, that this is not the true quota. See p. 154.

† From a report by Mr. Robt. Lytton, Her Majesty's Secretary of Legation, on the election of representatives for the Rigsraad, 1863.

says, this "shall be decided in such a way as to secure the representation by the candidate in question of all those who would not otherwise
be represented at all.   The remaining votes not needed for his return,
to be disposed of by lot or otherwise."   The latter seems to be a favorite
resource of the authors of some of the methods which have been devised.   But the admission of any fortuitous conditions whatsoever into
our electoral machinery should be condemned.   The sovereign will of
the qualified voters should be and is the governing power in republics,
and is the only power to which we owe allegiance.   Once give the
goddess of chance dominion even to a limited extent, and the consequences are not easily foreseen.

It would lead too far to attempt an analysis of the various "quota"
schemes of voting which have been proposed, but that the objection
which has been pointed out exists in some, if not all, of them has been
indicated by other writers on this subject from whom a few quotations
will be given:

In answering this objection* some of the friends of the system,
known as "the Single Transferable Vote," say: "The second votes
will *in general* be given to candidates of the same party with those
named first on the same papers.   Therefore the chance will not operate
as between party and party, but, which is much less important, as between different candidates of the same party.

"Moreover, *the chance* will operate within very narrow limits on
such large numbers as will have to be dealt with."

That the element of chance does exist with this system it will be
seen, is freely admitted by its advocates.

Mr. Alfred B. Mason, in writing of the Hare system,† said:
"There are three grave objections to this admirable scheme.   First,
in transferring votes the wishes of very many of the electors may be
wholly ignored.   *   *   *   In every election the element of chance
is introduced and the element of choice correspondingly disregarded."

* "Proportional Representation : Objections and Answers." By Sir John Lubbock,
Bart., M. P. ; Leonard Courtney, M. P. ; Albert Grey, M. P., and John Westlake, Q.
C   *The Nineteenth Century*, February, 1885.

† A New Theory of Minority Representation. *The New Englander*, July, 1874.

Mr. Frederick Seebohm, in the *Contemporary Review* for December, 1883, says :

" Mr. Hare's system, even as modified by Mr. Parker Smith, is understood by nearly all practical politicians to be too complicated, *and to leave too much to chance.*"

The writer in the *American Law Review* of January, 1872, referring to the Hare and the Free List Systems, says :

" The process of counting the votes, involving as it does a continual transferring of ballots, is not easy to follow in imagination, and is likely to present to the mind that does not fully enter into it, the aspect of an ingenious juggle or hocus-pocus that somehow produces in the hands of skillful persons most unexpected results, and that could, probably, in the hands of men yet more deeply skilled be made to produce any results they might desire. Moreover, the conspicuous existence of an arbitrary and fortuitous element, *in that the order in which the ballots are counted may materially affect the result,* although not displeasing to the philosophical mind, which recognizes the fact that a problem involving so many variable quantities must, in the nature of things, admit of a number of solutions all equally satisfactory, may naturally be a source of annoyance and distrust to the every day citizen."

Mr. G. Shaw Lefevre, referring to the system known as the Single Transferable Vote says : " It would be a mere chance which of the candidates other than the one whose quota is first filled, would be the unsuccessful one on either side, for there is no provision for taking into account the order of the preference on the papers used in making up the quota of the first or other candidates on the list, and the result might be very materially affected if the order of preference on these earlier and more numerous papers, were taken into account."

Miss Catherine H. Spence, of Australia, one of the latest advocates of what she called " Effective Voting," in a paper read before the World's Proportional Representation Congress in Chicago last summer (1893), said of The Single Transferable Vote that it " gives that accurate measure of the proportional strength of the two main parties and of outside parties which is so desirable. The contention as to the element of chance with regard to surplus votes *must be met by laying down strict rules which apply to all.''* This is a virtual admission of the charge that *chance* is an element in the system advocated, and that "strict rules'' are needed to "meet'' this difficulty. Apparently after the exercise of the ingenuity of many writers on this system for a quarter of a century or more, this fortuitous element has not yet been entirely eliminated from the system which Miss Spence advocated with so much ardor.

In a paper by Mr. William H. Gove, of Salem, Mass., which was read at the same congress, the author said of the Hare system :

"The novelty and comparative complexity of the Preferential Vote would render its adoption very difficult, and if adopted it would work unsatisfactorily because so few would mark more than one or two names, or mark them so as to distinguish between them.

"The second objection is the danger of a fraudulent count, which cannot be detected by the public or in any other way than by a recount.

"Suppose one hundred votes cast showing a first choice for X, fifty of whom show A as second choice, and fifty show B as second choice, and that fifty of $X's$ votes are to be transferred as a surplus. Then, although the votes to be transferred are selected by lot, as the system intends, and although any one selection by lot may hardly produce a materially different result from any other selection fairly made in the same way, it is plain that unfair enumerators might, by selecting the votes to be transferred, turn over all the fifty surplus votes either to A or B as they might choose, and thus the result might be very seriously affected. The suspicion of this, even if in most cases groundless, is in itself a strong objection to a system which justifies it. And it is to be observed that this objection has the more force where the ballot is secret, and did not arise to so great an extent in the original plan proposed by Thomas Hare in which the ballots were to be openly given, signed by the respective voters and preserved after the election for public inspection.''

At the meeting of the Proportional Representative Congress which was held in Chicago last summer a number of systems for securing proportional or minority representations were presented and considered. Two of those were approved by action of the Congress, and therefore it may be inferred that they were the most satisfactory plans proposed by the friends and advocates of the principles which were there discussed, and who were present at those meetings. Inasmuch as the system of election proposed by Doctors Burnitz and Varrentrapp has been explained and proposed as a substitute for cumulative voting, and it is thought would obviate most if not all of the defects of the latter system, a comparison and analysis of the three plans may help to indicate which of the three comes nearest to being "a thoroughly satisfactory scheme." With this object in view they are printed on the following pages and for convenience of reference are numbered I, II, and III.

I.

GOVE SYSTEM OF ELECTION.

An Outline of a Bill for the Election of Representatives in Congress According to the "Gove" or Single Transferable Vote System, One of the Two Systems Endorsed By the Proportional Representation Congress in Chicago, August 12, 1893:

Section 1. The members of the House of Representatives shall be elected at large in their respective states.

Sec. 2. In any state a ticket composed of as many candidates as the number of representatives which said state is entitled to choose may be nominated by any body of voters whose numbers equal one per cent. of the total vote cast for such representatives at the last preceding election, or by a petition of the same number of voters; and a ticket composed of a smaller number, or of a single candidate, may in like manner, be nominated by a smaller number of voters. But no voter shall join in the nomination of more than one such ticket.

Sec. 3. At any time after his nomination and not less than three weeks before the day of election, any of said candidates may furnish to the secretary of said state a statement in writing signed by himself and acknowledged before any official authorized to take acknowledgment of deeds, which statement shall contain the names of one or more others of said candidates with whom he believes himself to be in accord on the most important public questions, and to one or more of whom he wishes to transfer any ineffective votes cast for himself. And all such statements shall be published for the information of all voters in convenient tabular form not less than two weeks before the day of election, and said statements shall be opened for the inspection of the press and public generally as soon as received.

Sec. 4. Every legal voter shall be entitled to cast his vote in favor of any person eligible to said office. No person shall vote for more than one candidate. And every candidate receiving a quota of votes, to wit, the number obtained by dividing the total vote cast by the number of representatives to be chosen, shall be declared elected.

Ineffective votes shall be transferred according to the request of the candidate for whom they were originally cast to a person named in the list, if any, furnished by said candidate as provided in section 3.

SEC. 5. The following shall be deemed ineffective votes and shall be transferred in the order named.

1. Any votes cast for a candidate in excess of a quota as defined in Section 4, beginning with the candidate receiving the largest vote and proceeding to the one next highest and so on.

2. Votes cast for candidates who have since their nomination died or become ineligible, in the same order.

3. Original votes cast for candidates who received the smallest number of votes, beginning with the candidate having the smallest total vote and proceeding to the one next lowest, and so on, until the number of candidates whose votes have not been transferred as far as possible added to those who have received a quota equals the number of representatives to be chosen. Thereupon these shall be declared elected.

SEC. 6. Every ineffective vote of a candidate shall be transferred to the candidate named in his said list, living and eligible at the time of counting the vote, for whom the largest number of votes were originally cast and whose vote by transfer or otherwise does not equal the total vote cast divided by the number of representatives to be elected, hereinbefore defined as the quota. If the same number of votes were originally cast for two or more candidates named in said list, the candidate residing nearest the one from whom the votes are to be transferred shall be preferred.

SEC. 7. In case a vacancy shall occur in the delegation of representatives from the state after election, any ineffective votes which have been assigned to the member whose seat shall have become vacant shall be returned to the candidate for whom they were originally cast, and so many of those as are not then effective, together with the votes originally cast for said member, shall be redistributed to candidates who previously failed of election in the same manner as if said member had died or become ineligible before canvassing of the votes, and the candidate not before elected who shall then appear to have the largest number of votes shall be declared elected.

II.

FREE LIST SYSTEM OF ELECTION.

AN OUTLINE OF A BILL FOR THE ELECTION OF REPRESENTATIVES TO THE UNITED STATES CONGRESS, BASED UPON THE FREE LIST SYSTEM AS EMBODIED IN THE GENEVA LAW, AND THE BILL PROPOSED IN THE 52D CONGRESS BY THE HON. TOM F. JOHNSON, OF OHIO, ONE OF THE TWO SYSTEMS ENDORSED BY THE PROPORTIONAL REPRESENTATION CONGRESS IN CHICAGO, AUGUST 12, 1893:

SECTION 1. The members of the House of Representatives shall be voted for at large in their respective states.

SEC. 2. Any body of electors in any state, which polled at the last preceding congressional election one per cent. of the total vote of the state, or which is endorsed by a petition of voters amounting to one per cent. of such total vote, may nominate any number of candidates not to exceed the number of seats to which such state is entitled in the House, and cause their names to be printed on the official ballot.

SEC. 3. Each elector has as many votes as there are representatives to be elected, which he may distribute as he pleases among the candidates, giving not more than one vote to any one candidate. Should he not use the entire number of votes to which he is entitled, his unexpressed votes are to be counted for the ticket which he shall designate by title. The votes given to candidates shall count individually for the candidates , as well as for the tickets to which the candidates belong.

SEC. 4. The sum of all the votes cast in any state shall be divided by the number of seats to which such state is entitled and the quotient to the nearest unit shall be known as the quota of representation.

SEC. 5. The sum of all the votes cast for the tickets of each party or political body nominating candidates shall be severally divided by the quota of representation, and the units of the quotients thus obtained will show the number of representatives to which each such body is entitled, and if the sum of such quotients be less than the number of seats to be filled the body of electors having the largest remainder after division of the sums of the votes cast by the quota of representation, as herein specified, shall be entitled to the first vacancy, and so on until all the vacancies are filled.

SEC. 6. The candidates of each body of electors nominating candidates and found entitled to representation under the foregoing rules, shall receive certificates of election in the order of the votes received, a candidate receiving the highest number of votes the first certificate, and so on ; but in case of a tie, with but one vacancy to be filled, the matter shall be determined by lot between the candidates so tied.

SEC. 7. If a member of the House of Representatives shall die or resign, or his seat become vacant for any reason, the remainder of his term shall be served by the candidate having the next highest vote of the body of electors to which such member belongs.

III.

BURNITZ SYSTEM OF ELECTION.

AN OUTLINE OF A BILL FOR THE ELECTION OF REPRESENTATIVES TO THE UNITED STATES CONGRESS, BASED UPON THE SYSTEM PROPOSED BY DOCTORS BURNITZ AND VARRENTRAPP.

SECTION 1. The members of the House of Representatives shall be elected on a general ticket in their respective states.

SEC. 2. In any state candidates for election to the House of Representatives may be nominated by a petition of a number of voters for each candidate so nominated, equal to one per cent. of the quotient, obtained by dividing the total number of votes cast for such representatives in the state at the last preceding election, by the number of representatives to which the state is entitled, and cause their names to be printed in the official ballot. But no voter shall join in the nomination of more than one such candidate.*

---

* A suitable penalty to be fixed for a violation of this provision.

SEC. 3. Each qualified voter may give in his ballot the names of not exceeding ———* candidates for whom he votes and may indicate his preferences for such candidates by ordinal numbers marked opposite their names; or in the absence of such numbers the order in which the names are inscribed on his ballot shall indicate the order of his preferences.

SEC. 4. The first, second, third, etc., preferences for each candidate shall each be counted separately; the total number of first preference votes for each candidate shall then be divided by one, the total number of second preference vote by two, the third by three and so on. The quotients thus obtained for each candidate shall be added together and their sum will be his *elective quotient.* The———* candidates having the highest elective quotients shall be declared elected. A tie with but one vacancy to be filled shall be decided by lot.

SEC. 5. If a member of the House of Representatives shall die or resign, or his seat become vacant for any reason, the remainder of his term shall be served by the candidate having the next highest election quotient of the body of electors to which such member belongs.

The difficulty of understanding each of these three different schemes respectively will, it is thought, be apparent in reading them over. Their relative complexity is indicated to some extent by the fact that it has taken 710 words to describe the I. or Gove System of election, 453 for the II. or Free List System and 316 for the III. or Burnitz System. It is also thought that the series of measures, described in the latter method of voting, for computing the vote are much less involved and easier of comprehension by the ordinary mind than those of either the Free List or the Gove Systems.

In both of these schemes the method of calculating the quota given does not seem to be correct. It was shown by Mr. Droop in 1868 that the necessary minimum, or quota, of votes which is enough to make the election of a candidate certain is "*the number obtained by dividing the whole number of votes, given at an election, by the number of members to be elected, plus one, and increasing the quotient, or the integral part of the quotient, by one.* Thus if five members are to be elected and there are 36,360 votes, if we divide this number by 5+1=6 and we have 6060. Then 6060+1=6061=the elective quota. Any candidate securing that many votes will be elected no matter how his opponents votes may be combined against him.

The principles of the Gove system, were explained by its author

---

* The number to be elected.

at the Chicago Congress. In his paper, which was read there, he said that : " According to this system, each candidate, officially nominated, may file a list to be published with the nomination indicating such other candidates as he believes to be so far in accord with him that he wishes his ineffective votes to be transferred to some one or more of them. The transfer is then made, if necessary, to the one on this list needing it, who has shown the greatest personal popularity by receiving the largest direct vote.

" The voter knowing this list has only to select a single candidate and vote for him, and the thing takes care of itself ; he knows that if his vote cannot count for the candidate for whom it is cast, it will count for some other of the same general way of thinking. In voting he takes into account two things, the candidate and his list, just as he now regards the candidate and his party. And this plan is especially useful in cases where a candidate is independently nominated, as it leads him to declare his political affiliations, and thus inform the voter of the political position he assumes. It is true that the list of the candidates could ordinarily be made up by inserting the names of all other candidates of his party, but the parties would be smaller than now, either third parties or sub-parties prevailing, and when a party containing district elements had not divided into sub-parties, the same result would be obtained, as each candidate would be apt to place upon his list only the candidates of his own section of the party."

In voting under this system an elector would, in effect, be giving his vote to a candidate with the understanding, that if it was not needed or was ineffectual in electing that candidate, it was to be transferred to some other candidate, who was named before the election by the person voted for. Candidates having too many or too few votes to elect them would thus have a number of what, in effect, would be proxy votes, to be disposed of in accordance with their declaration made before the election. It seems difficult to foresee just what the effect of this would be in the hands of corrupt politicians and candidates nominated by and controlled by them. That it might be a prolific cause of evil, unless the transfer subsequent to the election was made compulsory and could be enforced by legal process, seems probable. That it might also be made a baneful instrumentality for making political bargains beiore the election is also to be feared. The election of all the members would, probably, not be decided by the direct votes of the electors, but by a secondary transfer of their votes to the candidates who were named by the persons voted for, as being "in accord with them on the most important public questions." There appears to be danger that the intentions of the voter might be diverted from his purposes by the transfer of his vote by one candidate to another. This plan undoubtedly would give representation to minorities, which would also be proportional to their numbers, which would be a great gain over our present method of electing representatives, and, if no other system was available, its adoption might be advisable.

The provisions of the II. or Free List system are at first a little puzzling. A voter has as many votes as there are candidates to be elected. He can give one of them to each of as many candidates as he chooses. These are counted for the candidates voted for. Then besides this *all* of his votes are counted for the *party* to which the candidates he has voted for belong. After the election all these party votes are divided by the elective quota which determines how many members that party is entitled to, and that number of candidates who have received the highest number of individual votes are declared elected. The same method is of course applied to the other parties.

This would also give minority and proportional representation to parties, and would thus be a great improvement over what we have now. It seems though besides being somewhat difficult to understand, to have what is perhaps a minor defect in not favoring independent voting within parties. This will be explained by an illustration :

It will be supposed that five members are to be elected in a district and that the Republicans have 18,183 voters and the Democrats 18,177, and that the regular Republicans have nominated *A*, *B* and *C* as candidates and the Democrats *F*, *G* and *H*, and that the voters cast their votes for the regular nominees of their parties, as follows :

REPUBLICANS.	DEMOCRATS.
A—18,184 votes.	F—18,178 votes.
B—18,183 "	G—18,177 "
C—18,182 "	H—18,176 "

As each voter can cast five votes for his party the Republican party would have $18,183 \times 5 = 90,915$ and the Democratic party would have $18,177 \times 5 = 90,885$ or a total of $181,800$. The true quota of this number would be ascertained by dividing the number of candidates $+1 = 5 + 1 = 6$ which will give $30,300$. Adding 1 to this $= 30,301 =$ the true quota, which divided into $90,915$, the vote for the Republican party, gives three as the number of members to which that party is entitled. Divided into $90,885$, the vote for the Democratic party, and we have only two, the number of members to which it is entitled. Consequently A, B, C, F and G would be elected.

Supposing though that there are 6061 Republicans who are not satisfied with A, B and C as candidates and consequently they nominate a fourth Republican, D, and have his name on the regular ticket and that they vote for him. As they each have five votes they would have a total of $30,305$—which is more than the quota. The vote for the different candidates would then be as follows :

REPUBLICANS.

A—12,123 votes.
B—12,122 "
C—12,121 "
D— 6,061 "

As there are the same number of Republican voters, who vote that ticket as before, the vote for the *party* would be the same as then, which would entitle it to three members, but as the three candidates who receive the highest number of *individual* votes are the ones selected to represent the party, A, B and C would still be chosen, although there is a quota of voters in favor of D, sufficient to elect him, by a correct system of election. The only way they could succeed then would be to run D on an independent ticket.

It seems very desirable that there should be freedom of voting within party *lines*, as well as that successful bolting should be made possible and that electors should be able to concentrate their votes effectually on any candidate, either within or without the party, whom they may prefer. This it is thought the Burnitz system of election will permit them to do, of which it may be said as Mr. Buckalew wrote of the cumulative system—although experience has not fully sustained his favorable opinion of it—that "it combines the advantages of other plans without their imperfections, while it is not open to any strong objection peculiar to itself. It will adjust itself to all cases, and it will have the most important and effectual sanction ; for it will be put under the guardianship of party interest, always active and energetic, which will give it directive and complete effect to the full and just representation of the people." *

* "Proportional Representation." By Hon. Charles R. Buckalew.

APPENDIX B.

A METHOD OF ASSURING TO THE MINORITIES AS WELL AS TO THE MAJORITY, AT ALL KINDS OF ELECTIONS, THE NUMBER OF REPRE-SENTATIVES CORRESPONDING TO THEIR STRENGTH.

Described by GUSTAV BURNITZ, PH. D., and
GEORGE VARRENTRAPP, M. D. Frankfort on the Main. 1863.

(Translated by Frank Weitenkampf.)

On the occasion of the various attempts at a constitutional change in Frankfort, a proper method of electing representatives always proves a special difficulty ; even within the same party an agreement was not effected, neither formerly nor at present. The wish to contribute to a solution of this difficulty, was the principal cause that prompted us to seek for a law by which the number of representatives obtained by the various parties would be in proportion to the number of their members. We believe that we have found this law, a law which preserves its validity in all kinds of election. We recommend it for trial.

As soon as any association of individuals,—social or scientific, re-ligious or political,—has become too numerous to manage its affairs itself or even only to control such management itself, it finds it necessary to transfer its authority to a smaller number of representa-tives. The election of these representatives is therefore an important action of far-reaching results. In all sorts of communities, if they are sound and vigorous at all, this importance is recognized. It will be regarded as a proper and suitable election of representatives if, in the corporate body elect, the opinion of the majority of those convened for election preponderates, and if the men of most ability and integrity obtain a seat and vote in the same. It does not lie within the sphere of legal provisions to see that the voters really cast their votes for the most suitable individuals ; education in general, and especially in the line of the community in question—*i. e.*, social, political, or other education,—will qualify and instruct for that purpose. On the other hand, the proper and genuine expression of the opinion and the will of the majority (for the good of the community) is, indeed, dependent upon proper ordinances and laws. The pursuit of this object has given rise to the most varying provisions. To speak, first of all, of elections in political communities : here,— with universal as well as limited suffrage,—elections in larger and smaller districts, elections according to rank, professions and classes, secret and public, direct and indirect elections have all been recommended. On none of these points has an agreement been arrived at.

Improvement of the election laws is striven for everywhere, even apart from the prime and most important endeavor to keep unauthorized influences away from the elections. In this effort we seem, at present, to have arrived at a decided turning point, which at the same time, in our opinion, demonstrates a great advance. This is the following :

All honest and intelligent friends of liberty and truth have sought above all to realize the problem of assuring to the majority of the voters a majority of the elect. But numerous difficulties, varying according to locality and other conditions, have hitherto permitted only incidental attention to the further problem of procuring representation also for the minority of the voters.

Hare, the first to observe this decidedly and clearly, developed it in his " Treatise on the Election of Representatives, Parliamentary and Municipal." Hare's system has been much discussed, especially among others, in Frankfort papers (" Zeit," December, 1861, Nos. 213 and 225, and " Frankfurter Reform," Nos. 58, 62, 65, etc.) But it found more opponents than advocates, nor has it as yet found practical application anywhere. To us it appears difficult, complicated, and indistinct. Cancelling and adding votes does not seem to be the right way of determining the relative worth which a party as· cribes to its various candidates.

If we desire to arrive at a proper solution of the difficult problem of producing a method of election which does not invade the liberty of the individual voter, which assures to the majority of the voters a majority of the elect, but at the same time makes provision for an, at least, approximately adequate representation of the minority, it will be well to begin with a consideration of the simplest conditions.

We therefore take a corporate body—purely social, religious, political or other—of 1000 persons as an example ; we furthermore assume that all the members agree in their opinions and purposes. It is incumbent upon this corporate body to appoint a representative. How will this corporate body proceed? It will convene and will undertake an inspection, or an estimation (*Werthschätzung*) of its members, in order to ascertain what person seems most suitable and capable to represent the corporation either in general or for a specified purpose. This proposed examination or estimation, in such a homogeneous corporate body as assumed, would presumably result in the casting of all votes for one person.   If a second representative, a third one, and so on, are then to be elected, one after the other, then, the conditions otherwise remaining the same, the renewed estimation will lead to the same result ; the united vote would again be given, to a second and to a third person.   All those elected in such manner have received the same number of votes, and yet these votes have not the same value in the sense of the voters, these votes in their equality in numbers do not correspond to the unequal value set by the voters upon the election of the first, second, and third elect.   For the second received his 1000 votes only because and after the first had already been elected, the third after the second, etc.   The value of seeing the second elected was a subordinate one in comparison with the value set on the election of the first.   This value or the prospect of the second, third, etc., was therefore only $\frac{1}{2}$, $\frac{1}{3}$, $\frac{1}{4}$, etc., as large as that of the first.   The following relation therefore appears :

$$1000 : \frac{1000}{2} : \frac{1000}{3} : \frac{1000}{4}.$$

These numbers,—which, in distinction from the votes received in reality by each one, and also in order to simplify matters, we shall call the *election-figures*,—correspond to the estimation which was set upon the individual by the corporate body, and thus makes clear the real will of the corporate body.

This estimation is more clearly apparent if the problem is inversely presented.   Again we take a corporate body of 1000 persons ; it had

hitherto elected 10 representatives at one election, and had unani-
mously given them each the same number of votes. As the unanimity
of the corporate body left no prospect of an electoral contest, the cited
estimation of the individual candidates did not appear necessary. But
now a change is produced through some circumstance or other, so that
the same corporate body has in future to appoint only 9 representatives instead of 10. It must therefore proceed to an estimation, although
in an inverse direction ; an agreement must be arrived at as to the one
among those ten men on whose election the least value is set. This is
repeated if the number of representatives is to be reduced to 8, 7, 6,
etc. ; an ascertaining of the least qualified continues to take place. Still
assuming a corporate body that is entirely in accord as to its views and
purposes, the question as to which of the former representatives is not
to be reëlected, now that their number is reduced, will of course be
decided with the same unanimity with which those to be elected were
formerly agreed upon. In both cases the number of votes was the
same for all the representatives, and yet the corporate body by no
means set the same value on the individual elections. The one who
was the last to be elected and the first to be removed was probably
rated at but one-tenth of the estimation in which the one first elected
was held.

This simple example, hardly likely to occur in reality, of a complete unanimity of all the members of an electoral body, has been
purposely presupposed in order to show that in each election an
estimation takes place, even though it does not become apparent
to the consciousness of the electors until the previous election
undergoes a change (diminishing, or the like). The conception of
the *election-figure*, as the expression of this estimation is therefore
founded in the nature of an election, and does not arise under certain
conditions only. This will appear more clearly yet at elections in
which various opinions stand in opposition to each other.

Each of the different parties existing in an electoral body will
nominate its own candidates when an election is to take place. What
was observed before in the homogeneous society is repeated in the separate parties : they muster their members and proceed to an estimation
of the same.

We will assume that there is 1 representative to be elected, and that there are three parties opposed to each other, one of which controls 1500, the second 900, the third 600 votes. Here, the candidate of the first party, receiving 1500 votes, is elected, and that justly, as the one on whom the highest measure of concurrence is concentrated. If a second election is then to be held,—closely drawn party-lines again resulting in a strict party vote of 1500, 900, and 600 for the different candidates,—the candidate of the first and relatively strongest party will again be elected, and so on in further elections, if more representatives are to be elected. The same result is arrived at if 3, 6, 10, or more representatives are voted for at *one* election; only the candidates of the strongest party will be victorious at the ballot-box; the minority, be it large or small, will always remain entirely without representation.

This takes place because only the number of votes cast is taken into consideration, and not the order of rank given by a party to its different candidates, in its relation to the relative strength of the separate parties. This relation changes, according as one or more representatives are to be elected.

1. At every election of one or more representatives by a number of persons, an estimation or valuation of those recommended for election—either in general or with a view to the attainment of some special object—will take place, consciously or unconsciously, and even within the same party. This estimation appears at the election in two ways: (*a*) by the number of votes cast for the individual candidate; (*b*) by the order of rank in which he is placed by his electors in relation to the other candidates nominated by the same party; this order of rank expresses the estimation set upon a candidate above the others of the same party, the measure of the chance of success which the party wishes to give one of its candidates above the others. Only at the election of a single representative do both estimations concur in *one election-figure.*

2. When several representatives are to be elected, and several parties differing in strength are opposed to each other, it is necessary clearly to show on the one hand the strength of the separate parties (that is, the number of votes bestowed by them on the individual candidates), and on the other hand the different estimation which the

separate parties set upon their individual candidates, and to contrast them in a proper relation.   This is done by means of the *election-figure* which results if the absolute number of *votes* received by a candidate is divided by the relative number of rank (*i. e.*, that given him on the different ballots).

If this law is put into effect, the majority of the voters will always eléct a corresponding majority of the representatives, but the minority will also receive the number of representatives corresponding exactly to its strength.

This will be made clear by some examples representing various party relations that occur, and at the head of which we place the example already referred to.   Three parties, of 1500, 900, and 600 votes, go to the ballot-box, and the following results appear.

Old method of counting.				*Election-figure* by ordinal rank.		
Candidate.	Party A.	Party B.	Party C.	Party A.	Party B.	Party C.
1st	1500	900	600	$\dfrac{1500}{1}=1500$	$\dfrac{900}{1}=900$	$\dfrac{600}{1}=600$
2d	1500	900	600	$\dfrac{1500}{2}=750$	$\dfrac{900}{2}=450$	$\dfrac{600}{2}=300$
3d	1500	900	600	$\dfrac{1500}{3}=500$	$\dfrac{900}{3}=300$	$\dfrac{600}{3}=200$
4th	1500	900	600	$\dfrac{1500}{4}=375$	$\dfrac{900}{4}=225$	$\dfrac{600}{4}=150$
5th	1500	900	600	$\dfrac{1500}{5}=300$	$\dfrac{900}{5}=180$	$\dfrac{600}{5}=120$
6th	1500	900	600	$\dfrac{1500}{6}=250$	$\dfrac{900}{6}=150$	$\dfrac{600}{6}=100$
7th	1500	900	600	$\dfrac{1500}{7}=214$	$\dfrac{900}{7}=128$	$\dfrac{600}{7}=85$
8th	1500	900	600	$\dfrac{1500}{8}=187$	$\dfrac{900}{8}=112$	$\dfrac{600}{8}=75$
9th	1500	900	600	$\dfrac{1500}{9}=166$	$\dfrac{900}{9}=100$	$\dfrac{600}{9}=66$
10th	1500	900	600	$\dfrac{1500}{10}=150$	$\dfrac{900}{10}=90$	$\dfrac{600}{10}=60$

etc.   etc.

According to this, the number of representatives obtained by each party would be:

	By old method of counting.			By the *election figure*.		
At an election	Party A.	Party B.	Party C.	Party A.	Party B.	Party C.
of 6 representatives.	6	—	—	3	2	1
" 10 "	10	—	—	5	3	2
" 12 "	12	—	—	6	4	2
" 16 "	16	—	—	8	5	3
" 20 "	20	—	—	10	6	· 4
" 25 "	25	—	—	13	7	5

Representatives.

For the second representative, the 900 votes cast by the second party for its first candidate already yield a higher *election-figure* than those cast by the first party for its second candidate, *i. e.*, 900 is more than $\frac{1500}{2}$; similarly, 600 is more than $\frac{1500}{3}$.

Now, if two parties—having respectively 60 and 38 votes for instance,—are opposed to each other, the following relation appears according to the two systems:

Old method of counting.			By the *election-figure*.	
Candidate.	Party A.	Party B.	Party A.	Party B.
1st	60	38	$\frac{60}{1} = 60.$	$\frac{38}{1} = 38$
2d	60	38	$\frac{60}{2} = 30$	$\frac{38}{2} = 19$
3d	60	38	$\frac{60}{3} = 20$	$\frac{38}{3} = 12.5$
4th	60	38	$\frac{60}{4} = 15$	$\frac{38}{4} = 9.5$
5th	60	38	$\frac{60}{5} = 12$	$\frac{38}{5} = 7.6$
6th	60	38	$\frac{60}{6} = 10$	$\frac{38}{6} = 6.3$
7th	60	38	$\frac{60}{7} = 8.5$	$\frac{38}{7} = 5.4$
8th	60	38	$\frac{60}{8} = 7.5$	$\frac{38}{8} = 4.7$
9th	60	38	$\frac{60}{9} = 6.6$	$\frac{38}{9} = 4.2$
10th	60	38	$\frac{60}{10} = 6$	$\frac{38}{10} = 3.8$

Thus, by the first count of votes, the second party remains entirely without representation ; by the sytem of computing *election-figures*, on the other hand, it receives one representative at an election of 3, 2 against 3 out of 5 representatives, 3 against 5 out of 8 representatives, 4 against 6 out of 10 representatives, 5 against 8 out of 13 representatives, or 2 out of 5, 3 out of 8, 4 out of 10, 5 out of 13.

The same result takes place when there is a larger number of parties :

Old method of counting. Party.				By the *Election-figure.* Party.			
A.	B.	C.	D.	A.	B.	C.	D.
1st Repre. 480	250	150	90	$\frac{480}{1}=480$	$\frac{250}{1}=250$	$\frac{150}{1}=150$	$\frac{90}{1}=90$
2d " 480	250	150	90	$\frac{480}{2}=240$	$\frac{250}{2}=125$	$\frac{150}{2}=75$	$\frac{90}{2}=45$
3d " 480	250	150	90	$\frac{480}{3}=160$	$\frac{250}{3}=83.3$	$\frac{150}{3}=50$	$\frac{90}{3}=30$
4th " 480	250	150	90	$\frac{480}{4}=120$	$\frac{250}{4}=62.5$	$\frac{150}{4}=37.5$	$\frac{90}{4}=22.5$
5th " 480	250	150	90	$\frac{480}{5}=96$	$\frac{250}{5}=50$	$\frac{150}{5}=30$	$\frac{90}{5}=18$
6th " 480	250	150	90	$\frac{480}{6}=80$	$\frac{250}{6}=41.6$	$\frac{150}{6}=25$	$\frac{90}{6}=15$
7th " 480	250	150	90	$\frac{480}{7}=68.5$	$\frac{250}{7}=35.7$	$\frac{150}{7}=21.4$	$\frac{90}{7}=12.8$
8th " 480	250	150	90	$\frac{480}{8}=60$	$\frac{250}{8}=31.2$	$\frac{150}{8}=18.7$	$\frac{90}{8}=11.2$
9th " 480	250	150	90	$\frac{480}{9}=53.3$	$\frac{250}{9}=27.7$	$\frac{150}{9}=16.6$	$\frac{90}{9}=10$
10th " 480	250	150	90	$\frac{480}{10}=48$	$\frac{250}{10}=25$	$\frac{150}{10}=15$	$\frac{90}{10}=9$
11th " 480	250	150	90	$\frac{480}{11}=43.6$	$\frac{250}{11}=22.7$	$\frac{150}{11}=13.6$	$\frac{90}{11}=8.1$
12th " 480	250	150	90	$\frac{480}{12}=40$	$\frac{250}{12}=20.8$	$\frac{150}{12}=12.5$	$\frac{90}{12}=7.5$
13th " 480	250	150	90	$\frac{480}{13}=36.9$	$\frac{250}{13}=19.2$	$\frac{150}{13}=11.5$	$\frac{90}{13}=6.9$
14th " 480	250	150	90	$\frac{480}{14}=34.2$	$\frac{250}{14}=17.8$	$\frac{150}{14}=10.7$	$\frac{90}{14}=6.4$
15th " 480	250	150	90	$\frac{480}{15}=32$	$\frac{250}{15}=16.6$	$\frac{150}{15}=10$	$\frac{90}{15}=6$

Thus, by the old method of counting votes the party A (numbering 480 votes), although it is weaker than the other parties put together, elects all of its representatives, no matter how many are voted for, while by our method of counting on the basis of the election-figure, representatives are elected as follows:

BY PARTY.

	A	B	C	D	
Of 10 Representatives,	5	3	1	1	Representatives.
" 12 "	6	3	2	1	"
" 15 "	8	4	2	1	"
" 20 "	10	5	3	2	"
" 27 "	14	7	4	2	"
" 36 "	19	9	5	3	"
" 46 "	23	12	7	3	"
" 57 "	28	15	9	5	"

If not only a few parties exist, but a separation into very many parties, a similarly just result is attained. Five hundred and fifty voters are divided into ten parties; and each has less than $\frac{1}{5}$ of the votes.

Party.

Representatives	A.	B.	C.	D.	E.	F.	G.	H.	I.	K.
1	100	90	80	70	60	50	40	30	20	10
2	$\frac{100}{2}=50$	$\frac{90}{2}=45$	$\frac{80}{2}=40$	$\frac{70}{2}=35$	$\frac{60}{2}=30$	$\frac{50}{2}=25$	$\frac{40}{2}=20$	$\frac{30}{2}=15$	$\frac{20}{2}=10$	$\frac{10}{2}=5$
3	$\frac{100}{3}=33.3$	$\frac{90}{3}=30$	$\frac{80}{3}=26.6$	$\frac{70}{3}=23.3$	$\frac{60}{3}=20$	$\frac{50}{3}=16.6$	$\frac{40}{3}=13.3$	$\frac{30}{3}=10$	$\frac{20}{3}=6.6$	$\frac{10}{3}=3.3$
4	$\frac{100}{4}=25$	$\frac{90}{4}=22.5$	$\frac{80}{4}=20$	$\frac{70}{4}=17.5$	$\frac{60}{4}=15$	$\frac{50}{4}=12.5$	$\frac{40}{4}=10$	$\frac{30}{4}=7.5$	$\frac{20}{4}=5$	$\frac{10}{4}=2.5$
5	$\frac{100}{5}=20$	$\frac{90}{5}=18$	$\frac{80}{5}=16$	$\frac{70}{5}=14$	$\frac{60}{5}=12$	$\frac{50}{5}=10$	$\frac{40}{5}=8$	$\frac{30}{5}=6$	$\frac{20}{5}=4$	$\frac{10}{5}=2$
6	$\frac{100}{6}=16.6$	$\frac{90}{6}=15$	$\frac{80}{6}=13.3$	$\frac{70}{6}=11.1$	$\frac{60}{6}=10$	$\frac{50}{6}=8.3$	$\frac{40}{6}=6.6$	$\frac{30}{6}=5$	$\frac{20}{6}=3.3$	$\frac{10}{6}=1.6$

According to this, the following number of representatives are elected by the separate parties:

	A.	B.	C.	D.	E.	F.	G.	H.	I.	K.
of 10 representatives	2	2	2	2	1	—	—	—	—	—
" 15 "	3	3	2	2	2	1	1	1	—	—
" 18 "	4	3	3	2	2	2	1	1	—	—
" 20 "	4	4	3	3	2	2	1	1	—	—
" 25 "	5	4	4	3	3	2	2	1	1	—

If it is thought right that the majority of the voters should decidedly have a majority, but not all, of the representatives, and that the
minority or minorities should also have a representation proportional
to their strength, then nothing is necessary but that, at elections at
which different parties are opposed to each other—be it for the election of a few or of many representatives—the voters, on casting their
votes, should show their relative preference for their different candidates, that is, on whose election they lay the greatest weight,
on whose election the second-greatest, on whose election the third-
greatest, fourth-greatest, etc.   For the moment this demand, because
unusual, will perhaps seem singular to one voter or the other, but if he
be a reasonable man, it will not be difficult to convince him of the
usefulness, nay necessity of the required valuation and classification ;
for without it a just and reasonable system of election is not possible.
But, certainly, only that system of election is just and reasonable the results of which give an exact impression of the views predominating in
an electoral body, which procures freedom and proportional representation for each opinion.   In future we shall no longer speak of an
"absolute removal of our opponents," or of "being ourselves absolutely removed," but of "representation of the different parties according to their strength."   Each party will strive, as heretofore, to induce
as many as possible of its members to vote, so that it may obtain as
many representatives as possible.   And if the majority acknowledges
the right of the minority to a proportional representation, and also
expects the minority to take a very active part in the election, it will
also recognize that it probably cannot elect all of its nominees, but,
out of 10 representatives, for instance, can count on only 8 or 7, perhaps only on 6 ; it must therefore make up its mind as to which of its
men it prefers, which first, which second, etc.   This valuation and
classification is made known by putting the candidates in this order
on the ballot, and no longer in alphabetical or other accidental order.
That is to say, not Alt, Becker, Christ, Dörr, etc., but :

1. Becker.	5. Alt.
2. Fritz.	6. Christ.
3. Haas.	7. Dörr.
4. Gerhard.	8. Engel, etc.

A well-disciplined party will come to an understanding as to such a succession, even though some sensibilities will be offended. But this will in no wise prevent the individual in the party from making some modifications in this succession ; by such alterations he by no means produces lost votes, nor does he, on the whole, change the result of the election, unless very many members of his party happen to be of the opinion that Mr. Alt, set down as No. 5 by the election-committee, had not been justly placed before Mr. Christ, set down as No. 6. Even so-called "mugwumps" or independents, who choose a few candidates from this and that party, will have a certain influence on the election, inasmuch as they only reach a certain number, and really take such names from the various parties, to which a certain prominence has already been given by their own parties.

As regards the unavoidable irregularities in an election on a large scale it is simply necessary to say that the present system is by no means tied down to the regularity which has been followed in these examples for the sake of clearness, but that it can, in fact, be applied just as well to the most scattering and various conditions of election, if only its underlying principle is adhered to, *i. e.*, that each candidate receives an ordinal number or order of preference which makes it possible to compute his *election-figure*.

This method of counting votes is furthermore equally applicable, valid and just, in the most diverse systems of election, in direct and in indirect election, with universal suffrage or an elective franchise limited by census, etc., in elections by ranks or classes. This seems hardly to require further elucidation. In larger countries the electoral districts are usually so distributed that only one representative has to be elected in each ; then the geographically different organization of the population (agricultural and manufacturing districts, mercantile cities, different denominations, and the like) usually procures currency for the difference of interests and opinions, at least to a certain degree. It should be determined, moreover, when a more just count of votes becomes possible, if it would not be better to enlarge those election districts, in which several representatives must be elected, consider-able minorities would then be sure of some representation, which they lack entirely under the present systems of election.

This method of counting, as is easily seen, commends itself, not only at the general elections of deputies, but also at the election of larger committees in the chambers of deputies themselves, in clubs, etc., in short, everywhere where minorities are opposed to a majority. Such committees would in future offer an exact and just image of the various parties in the chambers.

Only when due representation is given in such manner to the minorities, do provisions such as the one that at least two-thirds of the votes must be cast for an intended constitutional change, attain their true significance.

No matter where this method of counting is applied, no difficulty will ever arise. The officers of election will simply have a slight increase of work. Beside tabulating the returns, which must be performed with the greatest exactness, they must do a number of sums in division ; their services will perhaps be required for a day longer than formerly. But this extra work and the attendant expense (a day's pay for computers) are so inconsiderable in comparison with the great object aimed at, that a thorough discussion of this point seems hardly necessary.

An elucidation of the defects in the systems of election existing in the various countries, and of the improvement which might be effected in them by our method of counting, would lead too far. Every attentive reader, who is acquainted with the election-laws of his country, will be able to institute such a comparison for himself. By way of example, however, we will examine at least two election-laws more closely : that of a small state, the defectiveness of which has long been acknowledged by all its citizens, but which has still not been improved, simply because no one has offered a satisfactory substitute (Frankfort, free city), and that of Germany, such as it was proposed in the reform-bill as a method of chosing delegates.

In Frankfort every citizen is entitled to vote, and the citizens are divided into three classes : 1. scholars, artists, officials, etc. 2. commercial men. 3. tradesmen. The city forms only *one* election-district. Every year each citizen chooses 25 citizens in his own division ; the 75 delegates thus chosen then, by a majority of votes, elect 57 deputies. This is not the place to examine whether the kind,

number and size of these classes are proper ; we simply accept them
as an existing fact.   Now what is the result of such a class-election?
Various contingencies may arise here, all of which have a pretty
equally defective result.   In describing these contingencies we prefer-
ably cite such as have really occurred here.

1. In all three classes, one party (it may be, for instance, the old
liberal) preponderates, it therefore elects the 57 representatives from
its midst, and the minority remains wholly unrepresented.   This is
the case even when the majority is only a relative one, that is, if it
numbers 2000 votes for instance, while the democratic and the conservative parties control 1500 votes each.

2. A still more defective result is obtained if the two extreme parties, in order to overthrow the central party, wish to combine and
enter into a compromise which is opposed to the fundamental principles of each.

3. If the old liberal party has been victorious in two divisions,
and the democratic in the third, the 50 old liberal electors elect all
the deputies from their own party, and the 25 democratic delegates
have no influence whatever.

4. If the old liberal party is victorious in the second division, and
the conservative in the third, while in the first they are so close to
each other that the old liberals number 13 and the conservatives 12
delegates, then 38 old liberals will confront 37 conservatives on the
day of election of deputies, and if they be well-drilled partisans, the
former will elect all the deputies.   But what takes place ?   A delegate
of the second division (an old liberal) falls ill, the first deputy-dele-
gate of this division of course belongs to the conservative party, and
now in reality the opposite takes place, only conservatives being
elected.   This took place on October 28, 1850.

5. Or the old-liberals are victorious in the first-class, the democrats in the second, the conservatives in the third.   Each party has
25 electors; but at least 38 votes are necessary for the valid election
of a deputy.   In this case a defective compromise will finally lead to
a result that can hardly be good.

By way of remedy, direct election and a larger number of districts were recommended.   But such districts would be created quite

arbitrarily and fortuitously; no districts are to be formed here which represent different social interests. It is not possible to form classes according to property or taxes, as no census ever existed here. But if our method of counting should find favor, the one-election district might very well be continued, and all classes disregarded. Neither direct nor indirect elections are in any way anticipated; in the one as in the other, the method of determining *election-figures* will assure adequate representation to a minority or several minorities.

It is also not our business here to examine the political side of the delegate-project. Though it be in itself more proper than direct election, though it alone be able to prevent dissension between the various country representations and the national representation, though there be nothing else possible to Austria, all of which has been repeatedly asserted by the friends of the delegate-project, at all events it will be conceded that an unavoidable, nay, necessary and therefore irremediable defect of the same consists in this, that the representation of each country will only send its majority to the house of delegates, nay, that in the proper interest of the party it cannot act otherwise, because it must expect a similar proceeding with regard to the other country representations in which the opposite party has the majority. Thus, at present, the Prussian chamber of deputies would doubtless send no feudalists or clericals, the Bavarian one none of the progressive party, that of Wurtemberg none favoring smaller Germany, Nassau and Darmstadt no "greater Germany" men. Thus, as an authority on political science has more fully shown, the members of the convention of delegates would, it is true, be grouped according to political views, but this would be attended by no sort of mixture of the separate countrymen. The division by states would therefore make itself felt primarily, and such a convention would very probably further a particularistic separation of the citizens of the individual German states, while it really ought to form a most important medium for combination and amalgamation. All these disadvantages are completely done away with as soon as the method of counting by *election-figures*, as recommended, is introduced at the election of representatives of the countries for the convention of delegates. Then the Prussian feudalists and clericals, as well as the Bavarian progressive party, would be sure to send their adequate contingent to the convention of delegates.   Of course, this universal representation of the various parties, corresponding to their relative strength, would be still more complete, if the same method of counting had already been followed at the election of the deputies in the individual states.

The result of the proposed method of counting may, according to the preceding, be summarized as follows :

(1) The parties existing in a population find their original relative strength in the representation obtained on the basis specified.

(2) The minorities are adequately represented, while all the rights of the true majority are preserved ; the latter will decide at every vote.

(3) Each party is represented by those members which it holds in highest estimation.

(For mathematical demonstration see next page.)

MATHEMATICAL DEMONSTRATION.

Let a be the number of votes received by the candidate of the 1st party.

" b   "   "   "   "   "   "   "   "   "   "   " 2d "

" c "   "   "   "   "   ,"   "   "   "   "   " 3d "

" n "   "   "   "   " all the representatives to be elected.

$\left.\begin{array}{c} x \\ y \\ z \end{array}\right\}$ the number of the candidates elected by the separate parties.

The electoral lists, placed side by side, will, according to this, appear as follows :

and

$$\begin{array}{ccc} a & b & c \\ a & b & c \\ \hline 2 & 2 & 2 \\ \hline a & b & c \\ \hline 3 & 3 & 3 \\ \hline a & b & c \\ \hline 4 & 4 & 4 \\ \vdots & \vdots & \vdots \\ \hline a & b & c \\ \hline n & n & n \end{array}$$

$$\frac{a}{x} = \frac{b}{y}$$

$$\frac{b}{y} = \frac{c}{z}$$

$$x + y + z = n$$

1) $\dfrac{a}{x} = \dfrac{b}{y}$

   $x = \dfrac{ay}{b}$

2) $\dfrac{b}{y} = \dfrac{c}{z}$

   $z = \dfrac{cy}{b}$

3) $\dfrac{ay}{b} + \dfrac{cy}{b} + y = n$

   $ay + cy + by = bn$

   $y = n \left\{ \dfrac{b}{a+b+c} \right\}$

4) $\dfrac{a}{x} = \dfrac{b}{n \left\{ \dfrac{b}{a+b+c} \right\}}$

   $x = \dfrac{na \left\{ \dfrac{b}{a+b+c} \right\}}{b}$

$= n \left\{ \dfrac{ab}{a+b+c} \right\}$

$= n \left\{ \dfrac{a}{a+b+c} \right\}$

$$5) \quad \frac{b}{n \left\{ \dfrac{b}{a+b+c} \right\}} = \frac{c}{z}$$

$z = nc \left\{ \dfrac{b}{a+b+c} \right\}$

$= n \left\{ \dfrac{cb}{(a+b+c)b} \right\}$

$= n \left\{ \dfrac{c}{a+b+c} \right\}$

consequently

$x = n \left\{ \dfrac{a}{a+b+c} \right\}$

$y = n \left\{ \dfrac{b}{a+b+c} \right\}$

$z = n \left\{ \dfrac{c}{a+b+c} \right\}$

The strength of the original parties, however, reduced to n, is shown in the following formations :

1) $a+b+c : a = n : x$

   $x = n \left\{ \dfrac{a}{a+b+c} \right\}$

2) $a+b+c : b = n : y$

   $y = n \left\{ \dfrac{b}{a+b+c} \right\}$

3) $a+b+c : c = n : z$

   $z = n \left\{ \dfrac{c}{a+b+c} \right\}$

Hence it appears that the *election-figures* correspond exactly to the relation of the parties to each other.

APPENDIX C.

ELECTION BY PREPONDERANCE OF CHOICE.

By Dr. L. B. Tuckerman, Cleveland, Ohio.

The following interesting paper on this subject was also among those which were read at the Proportional Representation Congress held in Chicago last year (1893), and is reprinted from the *Proportional Representation Review* for September of that year:

In the city of Cleveland, Ohio, the elements composing the labor party have worked out a method of their own for securing proportional representation in caucuses and conventions, and for avoiding deadlocks where only a single person is to be nominated. The work cannot be said to be wholly that of any one person, all have contributed to the result, suggesting improvements here and eliminations there till we have developed a method which practically is found to work easily and satisfactorily. The method, which I shall call "The Cleveland Method," is based on the idea of preponderance of choice—a first choice does and ought to outweigh a second choice, a third, and so on; and this preponderance is expressed in numerals according to a perfectly simple rule which any person of ordinary intelligence can apply without difficulty. The rules are as follows:

1. Each voter will write on his ballot as many names as there are persons to be chosen, writing the names in the order of his choice; first choice, first; second choice, second; and so on. When nominations are made before balloting it is more convenient to write them on a board where all can read them.

2. In tallying the vote the tellers will read the last name on each ballot, first, crediting that name with one tally; the name next to the last, second, crediting the same with two tallies; and so on, always crediting the name written first on each ballot with as many tallies as there are names written on that ballot.

Thus a ballot written:
would be read: Coleman, one; Fetzer, two; Jones, 3; Brown, four; Smith, five.

Smith.
Brown.
Jones.
Fetzer.
Coleman.

And if a voter fails to write as many names as he is allowed to, no variation is made in the method of tallying—the voter simply loses so much of his vote, which he has a right to do if he chooses—the last name still counts one tally, the next to the last, two, and so on.

3. The person receiving the highest number of tallies is first declared elected ; the person receiving the next highest, next ; and so on until all the vacancies are filled. In case of a tie with but one vacancy to be filled, the incumbent is determined by lot.

The practical working of this rule (and we have tried it over and over again) is, that every element in the electing body large enough to have a quota, finds itself proportionately represented, and by its own first choice or choices.

Suppose, for instance, a caucus in a ward containing one hundred voters. They are to choose delegates to a convention. Suppose there are two factions, one counting on 55 voters and the other 45, and the contest so lively that a full vote is polled. Suppose further, that the first faction decides to support *A*, *B*, *C*, *D* and *E*, in the order named ; and the second, *F*, *G*, *H*, *I* and *K*, under the Cleveland method, the resulting ballot will tally as follows :

A,	55×5	275	F, 45×5	225
B,	55×4	220	G, 45×4	180
C,	55×3	165	· H, 45×3	135
D,	55×2	110	I, 45×2	90
E,	55×1	55	K, 45×1	45

The five highest are *A*, *F*, *B*, *G* and *C;* three of the majority faction and two of the minority—the first choices, the representative men of both factions. The advantage of this method in a caucus or convention is, that it reaches the result, certainly, directly and quickly, there is no counting the number of ballots cast and dividing by the number of persons to be chosen to find what the quota is ; there is no distribution of second choices, with the dissatisfaction that sometimes arises therewith ; the question whether the result would have been different had the ballots been counted in a different order. The ballots are tallied according to a simple rule the fairness of which commends itself to any man of ordinary intelligence, and the more sharply the lines are drawn between factions, the more nearly will each faction be found to have secured its exact proportion of the representation.

WHERE ONE IS TO BE CHOSEN. The three ballot rule.

1. A majority of the votes cast shall be necessary to an election.

2. In case no candidate receives a majority on the first ballot, a second ballot shall be taken in which each person shall express on his ballot his first choice and his second choice, by writing the two names in the order of his choice; a first choice tallies as one vote and a second choice as half a vote. A vote is not counted when the voter fails to express his second choice on his ballot as required.

3. In case no candidate receives a majority of the votes cast on the second ballot, a third ballot is taken between the two candidates receiving the highest number of votes on the second ballot, votes cast for other candidates being not counted.

To give an example of the working of the rule, suppose a congressional district containing five counties and aggregating 500 delegates in convention. Suppose the candidates before the convention, each county, of course, having a "favorite son," to be A, with 150 delegates pledged; B, with 150; C, with 100; D, with 60; and E, with 40. It only needs a little mulishness on the part of the delegates to deadlock such a convention indefinitely. Under the three ballot rule, however, the first ballot would stand as follows:

A, 150; B, 150; C, 100; D, 60; E, 40; 500 votes cast and no election.

On the second ballot, however, while each delegate would stand by his instructions or his pledge and vote for the same candidate as before, he must also express his second choice on pain of losing his vote altogether. And that second choice must be another of the candidates before the convention. Here individual judgment or preferences come into play and delegations solid for first choice will often divide on second choices. Suppose in this case A's supporters vote for E as second choice; B's divide, voting 50 for A and 100 for E; C's and D's going, say to E also, and E's to A, and likewise remembering that a second choice counts as half a vote, the second ballot would tally as follows:

A, 195; B, 150; C, 100; D, 60; E, 245; total, 750.

Again there is no election, no candidate has received a majority, but the preponderance of choice has designated two men ; A, with 195 votes, and E, with 245, as the two really prominent men before the convention. All the rest are dropped and the third ballot settles it between these two. Like the other rule it works certainly and quickly. Under it no charge of unfairness can arise, and there is no time for trades and dickers and no place for the bitterness and personal animosities that always remain after a long deadlock, a bitterness which not infrequently lays out at the polls the candidate who was finally successful in convention, even when the party whose nominee he is, has a substantial majority under ordinary circumstances.

[This method of election, it will be seen, is almost identical in principle with the Burnitz system. The difference being that instead of dividing the votes for different candidates by the numbers which indicate the order of their preferences, they are multiplied by the ordinal numbers arranged in the inverse order of preference. Thus the votes for the *first* choice candidate, when five are to be elected, is multiplied by 5, the second choice by 4, and so on, the fifth being multiplied by one. It does not seem as though this method distributed the elector's voting power correctly. If a voter has five votes which he can give or distribute among one or more candidates as he chooses, then he may give all five to one, but if he distributes them equally between two candidates then obviously the second can get only 2½ votes. In the illustration which the author of this paper has given the 55 voters might give 275 votes for A, but if they divide them equally between A and B, B would receive only 137½, instead of 220, which have been assigned to him. If this method of computing the votes is adopted it would seem as though the multipliers should be 5, 2½, 1⅔, 1¼ and 1, instead of 5, 4, 3, 2 and 1. The proposed multipliers would give exactly the same results as the Burnitz system, but it is much simpler to divide the total votes of the different orders of choice by 1, 2, 3, 4 and 5 than to multiply them by 5, 2½, 1⅔, 1¼ and 1.

The interesting facts stated in the paper, however, are that this method securing proportional representation in the labor party in

Cleveland was developed by the coöperation of a number of its members, and that the practical working of the system after many trials by a party composed of as many diverse elements as will naturally be found in the labor party of a great city like Cleveland has been satisfactory, and that since it has been adopted, every element in that party, large enough to have a quota, finds itself proportionally represented.]

APPENDIX D.

A BIBLIOGRAPHY OF MINORITY, PROPORTIONAL OR PERSONAL REPRE-
SENTATION, CUMULATIVE OR FREE VOTING, ETC.

[The following list of books, periodicals, addresses and magazine articles on the above and kindred topics has been prepared and is as full as the means and the time at command would permit, but no pretensions to completeness are made. As the writer knows no other language than his mother tongue—and that somewhat imperfectly—the reference to literature in foreign languages is, as will be seen, very limited. It is hoped, though, that this list, imperfect as it is, may be useful to those who want to extend their knowledge of the important subjects to which the publications enumerated refer. These have been arranged chronologically to indicate the relative positions in the order of the discussion which the different publications occupied. This arrangement, it was thought, would be the most useful to those who are studying these subjects

Acknowledgment should be made to the list of books published with Prof. Ware's article in the *American Law Review* of January, 1872, to a "Bibliography of Proportional Representation," by Prof. John R. Commons, in the *Proportional Representation Review* of December, 1893, and to Poole's Index. The author will be glad to receive any additional titles of books, essays or other publications relating to these subjects, which may be included in a more complete list here after.]

"The Representation of Minorities of Electors to Act with the Majority in Elected Assemblies." By Thomas Gilpin. Philadelphia, 1844. This is the first book published on the subject of proportional representation, though Norway, in the Constitution of 1814, seems to have been the first to make an attempt to give representation to the minority.

"De la Sincérité du Gouvernement Representatif, ou Exposition de l'Election veridique." Par Victor Considerant. Genève, 1846. Reprinted by the Swiss Society, Zurich, 1892. 15 centimes. Of historical importance, being the first brochure on proportional representation in Switzerland. The arguments have not been surpassed.

"A Disquisition on Government, and a Discourse on the Constitution and Government of the United States." John C. Calhoun. Edited by K. C. Cralle. Charleston, 1851

"Minorities and Majorities, Their Relative Rights: A Letter to Lord John Russell, M. P., on Parliamentary Reform." James Garth Marshall. London, 1853.

. "Minorities and Majorities, Their Relative Rights." James Garth Marshall. (Review of) *Edinburgh Review*, July, 1854. p. 116.

"The Machinery of Representation." By Thomas Hare. London: Maxwell, Bell-Yard, 1857.

"Parliamentary Government Considered in Reference to a Reform in Parliament." By Earl Grey. (Review of) *North British Review*. May, 1858. p. 43.

"On the Application of a New Statistical Method to the Ascertainment of the Votes of Majorities in a More Exhaustive Manner." Thomas Hare. Journal of the Statistical Society, September, 1860. p. 337.

"The Election of Representatives, Parliamentary and Municipal." First edition. Thomas Hare. London, 1859.

"Mr. Hare's Reform Bill Simplified and Explained." Henry Fawcett. 1860.

"Representation of every Locality and Intelligence." *Fraser's Magazine*. April, 1860. p. 536.

"Minority Representation, New Theory of." *De Bow's Review*. November, 1860. p. 631.

———————————————————— Thomas Hare. *Journal of the Statistical Society*. June, 1860. pp. 337, 347.

"Report of Select Committee of the House of Lords on the Franchise." June 26, 1860.

———————————————————— Thomas Hare. *Journal of the Statistical Society*. September, 1860. pp. 351-2.

"A Plea for a Pure Democracy." Miss Spence. . Pub. in South Australia, 1861.

"*Usque ad Cœlum*." Thomas Hare. p. 39. London: Sampson Low, Son & Co. 1862.

"De la Représentation des Minorités." M. Morin. Genève, 1862.

"True and False Democracy." Boston. Prentis & Deland. Congress Street, 1862.

"Suggestions for the Improvement of Our Representative System." By Thomas Hare. *Macmillan's Magazine*. February, 1862. p. 295.

"A Few Remarks on Mr. Hare's Scheme of Representation." By G. O. Trevelyan, B. A. *Macmillan's Magazine*. April, 1862. p. 480.

"Ideal of a Local Government for the Metropolis." Thomas Hare. *Macmillan's Magazine*. April, 1863. p. 445.

———————————————————— *North American Review*, Vol. XCV., 1862. p. 240.

"Considerations on Representative Government." John Stuart Mill. 365 pp. New York: Harper Bros. 1862. The chapter in this book on "True and False Democracy; Representation of all, and Representation of the Majority only," is one of the best statements of the reasons for giving minorities representation, ever published. Later editions of this book have been issued.

" The Degradation of our Representative System and its Reform." By J. Francis Fisher. Philadelphia. 1863.

" Methode, bei jeder Art von Wahlen sowohl der Mehrheit als den Minderheiten die ihrer Stärke entsprechende Zahl von Vertretern zu sichern." Dargestellt von Dr. phil. Gustav Burnitz und Dr. med. Georg Varrentrapp. Frankfort a. M. 1863. 16 pp. A translation of this pamphlet is given in pages 159–174.

—— —— —— —— —— —— —— —— *Christian Examiner.* Boston, 1863.

Report of Mr. Robert Lytton, Her Majesty's Secretary of Legation at Copenhagen, on the Election of Representatives for the Rigsraad. Presented by Command. 1864. (Printed in the London *Daily News*, Aug. 30-31, 1864; also as an appendix to a speech by John Stuart Mill on Personal Representation, delivered in the House of Commons May 29, 1867, and printed in pamphlet form, by Henderson, Raib and Fenton, Printers, 23 Berners Street, Oxford Street, London, 1867.) This report deals with the system as applied in Denmark, by Minister Andrae.

" Les Elections de Genève. Memoire Présenté au Conseil Federal et au Peuple. Suisse." Ernest Naville. Lausanne et Genève. 1864.*

" Conseil de l'Association Réformiste." Rapport du President. Ernest Naville. Genève. 1865.*

" Personal Representation." A Review of Hare's Election of Representatives. *Westminster Review,* Oct., 1865, p. 145.

" Individual Responsibility in Representative Government." Thomas Hare. *Fortnightly Review,* March 15, 1866. p. 350.

" Principles of Representation." Edward Wilson. *Fortnightly Review,* April 1, 1866. p. 421.

" Reform in our Municipal Elections." J. Francis Fisher. Philadelphia. 1866.

" The Election of Representatives, Parliamentary and Municipal." A Treatise by Thomas Hare. Third Edition. Philadelphia : J. B. Lippincott & Co. 1867. 350 pp. This is the most complete treatise on the subject to which it relates that has yet been published. Later editions have been issued since the first one.

" Personal Representation." *Nation,* Aug. 15, 1867.

" The Tyranny of the Majority." *The North American Review,* Jan., 1867. p. 205.

" Personal Representation." By David G. Croly, In *Galaxy,* July, 1867. p. 307.

" Report to the Constitutional Convention of the State of New York on Personal Representation." Prepared at the request, and printed under the auspices of the Personal Representation Society, by Simon Sterne. New York. 1867.

" Personal Representation." Speech of John Stuart Mill, M. P., in the House of Commons, May 29, 1867 ; with an Appendix, containing reports of Discussions and Publications in France, Geneva, Germany, Belgium, Denmark, Sweden, the Aus-

---

* The writings of Professor Naville are numerous, and besides giving remarkable exposi-- tions of the subject they are a complete history of the movement in Switzerland.

tralian Colonies, and the United States. London. 1867. Henderson, Raib & Fenton, Printers, 23 Berners St., Oxford St.

" Representative Reform. Report of the Committee Appointed by the Conference of Members of the Reform League, and Others, on Mr. Hare's Scheme of Representation." London. Trübner & Co. 1868.

" Les Minorités et le Suffrage Universel. Par le Baron de Layze." Paris. 1868.

" Del Potere Elettorale negli stati Liberi. Par Luigi Palma." Milano. 1869.

" Rapport de la Majorité de la Commission nommé par le Grand Conseil de la Républic et Canton de Neuchatel pour la Revision de la Loi Electorale, 1869."

" Report of the Select Committee of the United States Senate on Representative Reform." Government Printing Office, 1869. Reprinted in " Proportional Representation." By Senator Buckalew, Philadelphia.

" A Scheme for Proportional Representation." Walter Baily. London. 1869. Mr. Baily's system seems to be similar to the Gove System.

" Recent Discussions on the Representation of Minorities." *The Princeton Review* of October, 1869. p. 581.

" On the Political and Social Effects of Different Methods of Electing Representatives." By H. R. Droop. London. 1869.

" Constitution of the State of Illinois as Adopted in Convention, with an Address to the People." Chicago. 1870.

" Proportional Representation." David Dudley Field. *Putnam's Magazine,* June, 1870. p. 712.

" Representation Proportionelle de la Majorité et des Minorité." Par J. Borley. Paris. 1870.

" Teoria della Elezione Politica." Guido Padebetti. Naples. 1870.

" Le Suffrage Universel dans l'Avenir." Eugene Aubry-Vitet. *Revue des Deux Mondes* du 15 Mai, 1870.

" Representative Government. and Personal Representation." Simon Sterne. 237 pp. Philadelphia : Lippincott & Co. 1871. $1.75. An able presentation of the Hare System simplified and adapted to American institutions.

Proceedings of the American Social Science Association. The application of Mr. Hare's method of voting to the nomination of Overseers of Harvard College. New York. 1871.

Sessional Proceedings of the National Association for the Promotion of School Science, The School Board Elections. London. 1871.

" Memorandum on the History, Working and Results of Cumulative Voting." (Prepared for the information of the Belgian Government.) London. Printed at the Foreign office. 1871.

" The Cumulative Method of Voting." As exhibited in the late School-Board Elections. Birmingham. 1871.

" La Question Electorale." Par Ernest Naville.* Genève et Bâle. 1871. (A résumé of the publications of the Association Réformiste.)

---

* Refers to note on p. 182.

Proceedings of the American Social Science Association. The Application of Mr. Hare's Method of Voting to the Nomination of Overseers of Harvard College. New York. 1871.

Sessional Proceedings of the National Association for the Promotion of Social Science. The School-Board Elections. London. 1871.

"Minority Representation in Europe." T. Hare. *American Social Science Journal.* vol 3. 1871. p. 185.

"A Short Explanation of Mr. Hare's Scheme of Representation." By Millicent Garrett Fawcett. *Macmillan's Magazine.* April, 1871. p. 481.

"Minority Representation." *The Nation.* August 3, 1871. p. 69.

"Proportional Representation." C. R. Buckalew, ex-U. S. Senator, Penn. Edited by John G. Freeze. Philadelphia: William J. Campbell. 1872. 8vo. Price $3.00. Includes speeches, addresses, and report of the Senate Committee. Favors cumulative vote.

"Minority or Proportional Representation. Its nature, aims, history, processes and practical operation." By Salem Dutcher. New York: U. S. Publishing Co. 1872. 165 pp. Price $1.50.

"The Machinery of Politics and Proportional Representation." By Prof. Wm. R. Ware. *The American Law Review.* January, 1872. p. 255.

"Minority Representation." T. Gilpin. *Penn Monthly.* July, 1872. p. 347.

"Minority Representation." Simon Sterne. *Nation.* July, 1872. p. 69.

"Redistribution of Political Power." By E. H. Knatchbull-Hugessen. *Macmillan's Magazine.* November, 1872. p. 67.

"Proportional Representation." By S. Dana Horton. *The Penn Monthly.* June, 1873. p. 364.

"Réforme Electorale." M. Léon Petz de Thozé. Bruxelles, 1874. p. 8.

"Le Progrés de la Réforme Electoral en 1873." Ernest Naville. Genève, 1874.*

"A New Theory of Minority Representation." By Albert B. Mason. *The New Englander,* July, 1874. p. 573.

———— ——— ——— ——— ——— ——— ———— Leslie Stephen. *Fortnightly Review,* June, 1875.

"A Note on Representative Government." Thomas Hare. *Fortnightly Review,* July 1, 1875. p. 102.

"The Protection of Majorities or Considerations Relating to Electoral Reform." Josiah Phillips Quincy. Boston: Roberts Bros. 1876.

"Les Progrés de la Réforme Electoral en 1874 et 1875." Ernest Naville, Genève. 1876.*

"The Representation of Minorities." By Leonard Courtney, M. P. *Nineteenth Century,* July, 1879. p. 141.

"La Democratie Representative." Ernest Naville.* Genève et Paris. 1881.

"On Methods of Electing Representatives." H. R. Droop. *Journal of the Statistical Society,* June, 1881. p. 141.

---

* Refers to note on p. 182.

" The People's Power ; or How to Wield the Ballot." By Simeon Stetson. San Francisco : W. M. Henton. 1883. 63 pages, paper, 25 cents.

" Proportional Representation." (Italian.) Cav. Francesco, Sec. to the State Council. Rome. 1883.

" The English Radicals and Minority Representation." *The Nation*, October 25, 1883. p. 347.

" Minority Representation." J. Parker Smith. *Spectator*, November 10, 1883. p. 1444.

" The Minority Vote." *Spectator*. December 15, 1883. p. 1617.

" Proportionate Representation." By Frederic Seebohm. *Contemporary Review*. December, 1883. p. 905.

" Parliamentary Reform : Minority Representation." By J. Parker Smith. *Westminster Review*. January, 1884. p. 163.

" Proportional Representation." By Robert B. Hayward. *The Nineteenth Century*. February, 1884. p. 293.

" Proportional Representation : A Practical Proposal." By John Westlake, Q. C. *Contemporary Review*. March, 1884. p. 417. Also reprinted for the Proportional Representation Society.

" Representation and Misrepresentation." *Westminster Review*. April, 1884. p. 392.

" Proportional Representation." By Sir John Lubbock, Bart., M. P. *Nineteenth Century*. April, 1884. p. 703.

" A Test Election." By H. O. Arnold Forster. *Nineteenth Century*. April, 1884. p. 716.

" The Representation of Minorities." By G. Shaw Lefevre. *Contemporary Review*. May, 1884. p. 714.

" Proportional *vs.* Majority Representation." By Albert Grey, M. P. *Nineteenth Century*. December, 1884. p. 935.

" Fair Representation." Walter E. Smith. London : Kegan Paul, Trench & Co., 1885. 63 pages. Price (paper) 1s., cloth, 6s. A careful examination of various plans of Proportional Representation.

" La Democratie Representative. Representation Proportionelle de la Majorité et des Minorités." By Edouard Campagnole. Rue Soufflot, Paris, 1885.

" The D'Hondt System and the Single Transferable Vote." (Italian.) Florence. 1885.

" Representation and Misrepresentation. The Crusade for Proportional Representation." Thomas Hare. *Fortnightly Review*. February 1, 1885. p. 202.

" Proportional Representation : Objections and Answers." By Sir John Lubbock, Bart., M. P. ; Leonard Courtney, M. P. ; Albert Grey, M. P. ; and John Westlake, Q. C. *The Nineteenth Century*. February, 1885. p. 321.

" Practical Consideration on the Representation of Minorities." By I. Boyd Kinnear. *Fortnightly Review*. February 15, 1886. p. 49.

" Working Men on Minority Representation." *The Nation*. September 16, 1886. p. 229.

" Die Frage der Einführung einer Proportionalvertretung Statt des Absoluten Mehres." Bischoff Von Hagenbach. Basel, 1888.

" Le Suffrage Universal et le Régime Parlementaire." Par M. Paul Lafitte. 1889.

"Representation, Imperial Parliament, No. 2." 6th thousand. By Sir John Lubbock. London : Swan,. Sonnenschein & Co., 1890. 90 pages. Paper, 9d. A brief, clear discussion. Favors the single transferable vote. Sir John Lubbock is president of the English Proportional Representation Society.

" Bericht des Grossrats." Kommission über das Initiativbegehren betreffend Einführung der Proportionalvertretung, bei den Wahlen in den Grossen Rat. Basel, 1890.

" Congressional Directory Supplements, 1890 and following, Washington." Maps and population of all Congressional Districts for each Congress, beginning with the 51st. A telling object lesson.

" Representation Proportionalle des Opinions Differentes dans les Elections." Par J. Curie, Paris, 28 Rue Serpente, 1891.

" La Representation Vraie et la Revision." Jean Mommaert. Société Belge de Librairies. Bruxelles, 1891.

" The Gerrymander of Wisconsin." A. J. Turner. A review of the legislative apportionment act of 1891. The author. Portage, Wisconsin. 26 pages. Maps and statistics of a remarkable legislative gerrymander, since declared unconstitutional by the Supreme Court.

" Proportional Representation a Remedy for Gerrymandering." By Prof. John R. Commons. Philadelphia : American Academy of Political and Social Science. 1891.

"An Unrepresentative Congress." Stoughton Cooley. *Belford's*. December, 1891.

" A New Plan for Minority Representation." J. R. Commons. *Review of Reviews*. November, 1891.

" An Appeal to the Canadian Institute on the Rectification of Parliament." Sanford Fleming. Toronto : The Copp Clark Co., 1892. 173 pages. Contains announcement of prizes by the editor and well selected extracts from writers on party politics and electoral reform. Contains also the report of Lord Lytton on the election of representatives in Denmark.

" Legal Disfranchisement." Stoughton Cooley. *Atlantic Monthly*. April, 1892.

" The Slaying of the Gerrymander." Stoughton Cooley. *Atlantic Monthly*. May, 1892.

"How to Abolish the Gerrymander." J. R. Commons. *Review of Reviews*. December, 1892.

Cridge, Alfred.—" Proportional Representation. Including its relations to the Initiative and Referendum." San Francisco. 1893. Published by the author, 429 Montgomery Street. 10 cents.

"Proportional Representation." A series of 13 articles in *The Twentieth Century*, 19 Astor Place, New York, by J. R. Commons, beginning June 29, 1893.

" Proportional Representation." W. D. McCrackan. *Arena*. February, 1893.

" Proportional Representation." Stoughton Cooley. *New England Magazine.* March, 1893.

" Why Municipal Government Fails." Stoughton Cooley. *American Journal of Politics.* August, 1893.

Essays Received in Response to an Appeal by the Canadian Institute on the Rectification of Parliament. Toronto : The Copp Clark Company, Limited. 1893.

" Primary Elections. A Study of Methods for improving the Basis of Party Organization." Daniel S. Remsen. New York : G. P. Putnam's Sons. 1894.

PERIODICALS.

La Representation Proportionelle. Paris, F. Pichon, 1888. 524 pages, 10 fr. Published under the auspices of the Sociétié pour l'etude de la representation proportionelle of France. An able exposition of the reform by the secretary of the society, and a complete history of legislation in all countries.

La Representation Proportionelle Revue Mensuelle. Bruxelles, Belgium. Published since 1882. 5 fr. yearly. The organ of L'association Reformiste belge pour la Representation Proportionelle. Contributions from the foremost continental reformers. The volume for 1885 contains a full account of the international congress at Anvers.

Bulletin de la Société Suisse pour la Representation Proportionelle. H. Georg, librairie-editeure. Genève et Bâle, 1885. Prix du numero 50 centimes.

Hope and Home. Alfred Cridge, editor and proprietor. San Francisco. 25c. a year. Devoted to Direct Legislation and Proportional Representation.

The Proportional Representation Review. Published quarterly by the American Proportional Representation League of Chicago.

"THE PROPORTIONAL REPRESENTATION REVIEW."

CONTENTS OF SEPTEMBER NUMBER, 1893.

The Proportional Representation Congress.
Outline of Bill Based on Free List System.
Outline of Bill Based on Gove System.
Proportional Representation, Prof. John R. Commons.
Ticino as an Object Lesson, W. D. McCrackan.
Effective Voting, Catherine H. Spence.
The Gove System, Wm. H. Gove.
The Proxy System, Montague R. Leverson.
Majority Myths, Alfred Cridge.
The Solution of the Problem, T. Curie.
Preponderance of Choice, Dr. L. B. Tuckerman.*
Address of The American Proportional Representation League.

---

* See p. 175.

CONTENTS OF DECEMBER NUMBER, 1893.

Proportional Representation as a Means of Political Reform, William Dudley Foulke.
The Application.   Form of Ballot for the Four List System.
The Cumulative Vote, John Z. White.
Proportional Representation in Switzerland, Prof. Ernest Naville.
A Bibliography of Proportional Representation, Prof. John R. Commons.
State of the Movement.
Editorial Notes.

CONTENTS OF MARCH NUMBER, 1894.

Reform in City Government, Hon. Charles Francis Adams.
The Line of Least Resistance.
The Present Condition of the Proportional Representation Question in France, Lieut.-Col. J. Curie.
Proportional Representation in Belgium, Prof. John R. Commons.
State of the Movement.
Editorial Notes.

THE END

INDEX.

L H.
11/61